The Adventures of "Indiana" Hannebaum

The King of Metamora

The Adventures of "Indiana" Hannebaum
The King of Metamora

Harold W. Hannebaum

University of Idaho Press
Moscow, Idaho
1995

University of Idaho Press, Moscow, Idaho 83844-1107
Printed in the United States of America

00 99 98 97 96 5 4 3 2 1

Cover photo (left to right): Emmett W. "Bob" Jones, Oscar
Hannebaum, Harold "Indiana" Hannebaum, and William
Robert "Rob" Jones on the porch of Grandpaw Jones's house
in Franklin County, Indiana.

CONTENTS

The King of Metamora

One day I went into the Martindale store from school at noon, told them what I wanted, and simply signed my name for it. I thought this was great—I didn't need any money and could have anything I wanted!

I started acting like a king! I got lots of goodies simply by signing. Life was really wonderful, until the end of the month when my folks received their statement from the Martindale General Store.

After looking over their bill, Mom and Dad sat me down, and I had lots of explaining to do. When I tried to tell them how you didn't need money in the Martindale's store, I thought they were going to kill me for sure.

The rolling hill country where we lived in southern Indiana was probably one of the best places on Earth for kids to grow up, if they survived. The days were beautiful in every season, and the moonlit nights were full of real fun and adventure.

I was awful uncomfortable during the lessons inside the schoolhouse, but I loved to study everything else everywhere I went. It was an exciting time of secrets, new inventions and miracles for a young Hoosier like me.

And then suddenly, I found myself in the middle of the wild West!

— Harold W. "Indiana" Hannebaum
Sun Valley, Idaho

INTRODUCTION

My name is Harold Hannebaum, and most of my life has been spent inventing things. Right from the start I enjoyed a very interesting life.

I was born on January 6, 1910, on a beautiful one hundred and sixty acre valley farm near Metamora, Indiana, about forty-five miles below Indianapolis. John H. Hannebaum and Flora Nell Jones were my Dad and Mom.

As a young boy I always liked inventing and making my own toys. Any wheel that wasn't attached to something was always put to good use by me. I spent my young years running over the hills, climbing trees, fishing and swimming in the Old Whirl Hole on Pipe Creek that runs through my Dad's farm.

My Dad first married Molly Gloshen, a fine lady I never met. They had four sons: Clarence, Addie, Herman and Oscar. After Molly died in 1896, Dad's mother watched over his four sons a few hours each day, while Dad did his farming and worked to clear more land.

Dad married my Mom, Flora Nell Jones, in 1899. To them came six kids: Marshal, who died as a baby; then our only sister, Flora Mae—we always called her Dollie; Willie, who died at the age of nine; next Bert; followed by Lester—always Smart Ol' Lester to me; and finally me, being the youngest of my Dad's ten children.

In the early 1900s, Southern Indiana had been settled mostly by German immigrants. No matter where they came from, the farmers all seemed to be very particular about how their towns and farms looked, just like Dad.

The farmers in Franklin County operated their places very systematically. For example, they planted the lowlands and used the lower slopes of the hills for houses and livestock. They usually turned the hillsides into bluegrass pasture land, and used the tops of the hills for woodlands.

At my age those beautiful woodlands were like mountain-tops to me. The woodlands kept farm families supplied with firewood in the winter, cookstove wood the year around, and saw-logs for construction materials.

After doing some deep thinking, Dad decided to make a big effort to add more bluegrass pastures to his farm by clearing most of the timber from his hillsides. With the help of his four oldest sons and many hired men, they cut timber to create bluegrass pastures. Whenever I see a beautiful golf course, it reminds me of my Dad's hillside pastures.

Dad wasn't about to let any of his timber go to waste so he brought in a steam-engine-powered sawmill. As the lumberjacks cut and trimmed the trees, two men worked with oxen and horses to drag the saw-logs down the hillsides.

Then a four-man crew ran the timber through the fiery sawmill. In went rough logs and to my great astonishment, out came beautiful finished lumber of every length and every dimension needed for Dad's framing, siding, and roofing.

Two other men moved the sweet-smelling lumber to each of the building sites around the farm. Dad hired carpenters, plasterers, roofers, and cabinetmakers to work at the different building sites.

This work went on for months, with Dad acting as the boss and the foreman. He had to keep all the men and all the equipment busy, as this building project was costing a lot of money.

I was just a small boy at that time, and all of this commotion was very interesting to me. There was one man, however, who I thought was particularly amazing. He was the joiner who made the window frames, door frames and doors, and all of the other kinds and sizes of wooden parts that were most difficult. Almost every corner he made was precisely dovetailed.

This man did most of his work using just a few tools, including a square, handsaw, nail hammer, wood plane, auger, draw knife, level, miter box, gimlet, crowbar, foot edge, and a sharp hatchet. There were no power tools to make the job easier for him. To me his fine work was pure inventive magic and I learned a lot about craftsmanship just from watching him.

Dad's buildings used up nearly all the lumber sawed from the logs on his farm. This included our large seven-room house and our separate summer kitchen. The men built four tobacco barns located at various places around the farm, and another large livestock barn. The livestock barn included four hay mows, twelve stalls to hold twenty-four horses, a holding pen for twelve cows, three corncribs and twelve hog houses. Of the ten other buildings they built, the most important to me was the wonderful tool shop!

Dad's Metamora farm looked like a small town when he finally finished. People came from all over to visit and get ideas.

The hill country in southern Indiana where we lived was particularly beautiful, and it was probably one of the best places on Earth for kids to grow up.

I will never stop thinking about my exciting childhood there. I hope that you enjoy the adventures that I had with my family, my childhood friends and also the animal friends that I was always with whenever possible.

| 1 |

SMART OL' LESTER

If my parents thought my brothers and I were lost they first checked our many fishing holes. When they found us, we would explain to them that we were not lost. They would ask, "Then how come you missed your supper?"

Over and over we learned how awful it was to be sent to bed without supper, and even worse with a sore rear end. Our sister Dollie, however, always stayed close to home and only had to be searched for once.

While I was still a small kid, three of Dad's oldest sons left home, married, and started families of their own. They were Clarence, Addie, and Herman. This left Oscar, the youngest son from Dad's first marriage, still at home with Dad and his second family, including Mom, Dollie, Bert, Smart Ol' Lester, and me.

For years me and Lester had fun exploring all of the buildings on our farm. We were close in age and were young enough so we didn't have to work too hard.

One afternoon we decided to climb up on top of the house. We climbed a downspout, and when Dad spied us running back and forth up there he called us down and gave us a real going-over for being on the roof.

"A shingled roof is far too fragile to run around on," Dad lectured us. We escaped down to Pipe Creek as soon as we could get away.

"What does that word *fragile* mean?" I asked Smart Ol' Lester as we ran down the hill. Lester had just started school, and I knew that school was where you learned what strange words meant.

We both jumped into a water hole at the creek. Lester could swim, but I couldn't yet, so I stayed in shallow water. When he surfaced, I asked him again.

"Why don't you try to help me think?" he sputtered. "My head is just too tired from Dad's going-over to do *your* thinking and *mine*, too." This surprised me. Lester was two and a half years older than me and had always had good answers before.

We splashed around an awful lot. Then as we rested Lester chewed on a piece of farm tobacco—we didn't know any better in those days—while he did some deep thinking. Finally he said, "I think *fragile* means *slivers*. I got a couple of them in my rear end when I slid down up on the roof."

That strange word was clear to me at last. "I got some of them in my foot, too," I said, scratching at my heel. Lester's understanding of things was invaluable to me as I was growing up.

With that settled, Lester then went under the water long enough to cause me some concern. When he finally surfaced, he exclaimed, "I just saw a fish down there weighing himself, and he weighed four pounds!" I didn't believe him, so I said, "How did that fish know he weighed four pounds?" Lester was ready. He said, "Why, he used his own scales!" I buzzed my lips at him and tried to push him back under, but couldn't do it.

After awhile I began to notice I was hungry. "Lester, do you reckon it's time for us to head home for supper yet?"

"Just wait a minute," Lester said, "and I'll show you something." He began to search through last year's dried-up horseweed stems. Billions and billions of horseweeds grow along the banks of Indiana's creeks and rivers. Some of them grow up to twelve feet tall and their stems are completely hollow. Soon he found two long ones that he liked and snapped them off.

"Come here, Harold," he said, climbing out on the bank, "and I'll teach you the secret of when to head home for supper." Handing me one of the horseweeds, he showed me how to put one hand on top of my head, stand a stem on the ground in front of me, then break it off to measure exactly how tall I was.

Next he showed me how to stand with my back to the evening sun, draw a line in the dirt where I stood, then measure my own shadow on the ground with our horseweed stems. "This time of year when your shadow gets about two times as long as you are tall," he said, "then you know it's time to get home for supper. But if your shadow is four times your height, you better forget about supper and try to sneak in after dark to save Mom the trouble of giving you a whipping." I was puzzled and filled with admiration for my smart older brother.

"How did you learn about this secret?" I asked him in awe.

"Since the Indians had no calendars and no clocks, Little Brother, this shadow-measuring trick is how they kept track of the time of day and the seasons, too," he said. "I read about it in a book at school."

Both of our shadows were now more than two times longer than we were tall, so we started off running. We knew we would be punished if we stayed lost too long. And if we missed our supper, we knew Mom would throw our good food out to our dog Gussy and to Just Plain Cat, our tomcat without a name.

Tomorrow I would ask Smart Ol' Lester the other half of the Indian secret he had learned.

| 2 |

A BIG FLOOD

It was nearly noon before I remembered to ask Lester my question. "Say, Lester, how can Indians tell what season it is just by looking at their shadows?"

"I'm sorry, Little Brother, but I just can't tell you," he said.

"Then I'll go ask Bert. He has probably read the same book that you read at school."

"He won't tell you, either," he said, shaking his head. "But I *will* tell you why I *won't* tell you."

"Okay," I replied. That seemed better than nothing, and it might be a sign that Lester was weakening.

He leaned over very close to my left ear and in a hoarse whisper said, "Because it's a *secret*, dummy!"

Well, I made Lester's life miserable hour after hour until he finally agreed to let me in on the secret.

"Okay, *okay*, OKAY! I'll tell you the secret," he surrendered.

"But first you must promise to always keep it to yourself and never tell anyone else."

"I promise," I said eagerly.

"This is how. When you look at your shadow outside, if it falls on dry ground, it is usually summer. If it falls on colored leaves, it is usually fall. If it falls on snow or ice, it is winter. And when it is spring, the snow under your shadow is melting. Got it?"

"By golly, that makes sense!" I said. "So you can tell the seasons by what's *under* your shadow, and what time it is by how *long* it is!" Now I knew that Ol' Lester was the smartest brother in the whole world, and I loved him for passing along these precious Indian secrets to me.

A week later the rain poured down and flooded the Whitewater River near our home.

We had a fancy porch that ran around three sides of our white, two-story frame home. Our lawn was enclosed by a nice-looking fence. The main road ran along outside of our front gate.

Lester was busy running in and out of the house, but I mostly stayed hanging onto the front porch rails. As far as we could see, it was water, very muddy water with lots of things floating in it. In fact, it was *raging* muddy water.

I was frightened by the rampaging river, and also by the way my Mom, Dad, brothers, and sister were acting. They all seemed to be very excited and alarmed at what might happen if the floodwaters kept rising. I stood by myself and couldn't help thinking—a whole lake of hot chocolate! I loved hot chocolate.

Then I spotted a big barn rat swimming down the current in the road, heading for the gatepost in our front yard. I watched this poor ol' rat trying his best to make it. With one last great struggle, he heaved himself up onto the top of the post. I looked at this pitiful wet rat and wondered, "What will he do when the water rises up *over* the post?"

My brothers suddenly ran out onto the front porch. They were pointing up the road. I forgot about my poor wet rat and stared in amazement. In the past I had only seen horses and wagons on the road, but now I saw a rowboat coming the same way carrying Uncle Bob Jones and Uncle Harry Jones, two of my Mom's brothers. I was very happy to see them. Now I knew that everything would be fine.

"Flora, we thought we smelled your fresh apple pie," said my Uncle Bob, grinning, "so we rowed over to investigate." Mom gave them big hugs because she loved having her brothers visit for any reason.

We were all still gathered on the front porch looking out at the floodwaters when we spotted a big house floating down about where Pipe Creek used to be. It was a cloudy but warm day, and some people were sitting on top of the house. They began to yell and wave to us.

My two uncles jumped into their rowboat and rowed in the direction of the floating house to rescue the people. They rowed right over the telephone line to get to them.

I don't know what happened next to my poor wet rat or to those people on the rooftop or to my uncles as they chased down the big house in their little rowboat. I only know that I was happy when my uncles arrived back before dark and finally received their reward of freshly baked apple pie.

After the sun went down and we finished supper, we all stood out on the back porch watching in the twilight. We couldn't help but look in wonder at the now-calm floodwaters. Our outbuildings were completely surrounded.

Suddenly we heard a loud banging noise—one loud bang after another—coming from the direction of our tool shop. In fact, it was coming from *inside* the shop!

I was really frightened. So were Lester and the other kids, and maybe even Mom and Dad. This banging didn't stop, and none of us could understand it or what was causing it. It had a mysterious, numbing effect on everyone.

Dad finally said, "One of us will have to go down to the tool shop and investigate what this loud noise is." Everyone stood there for awhile wondering who might be brave and do the job.

After we listened to the banging for a long time, Oscar said, "I guess I will be the hero and save every one of us from that unknown thing."

I had thought that Oscar was the bravest of my brothers

anyway, and now I knew it. He slowly made his way through the darkening waters, with the light from a kerosene lantern circling mysteriously out from his hand toward the half-submerged tool shed.

When Oscar was almost there, the banging suddenly became much louder. Scared, Oscar turned around and headed back to the house, only to receive shouts of encouragement from the brave group still standing on the back porch.

Out there all alone, Oscar finally turned around and started to walk back toward the tool shop. When he and his light disappeared through the swinging shop door, I shivered.

Now lots and lots of banging was going on in the tool shop! I was so worried for Oscar. After what seemed like an eternity, he stumbled out through the swinging door, half-carrying and half-dragging something in his arms. Somehow Oscar's lantern stayed lit while he struggled toward the house. Boy, I was so happy to see that Oscar was okay, but I was also frightened by what he was carrying.

While he made his way toward the porch, the odd-looking thing violently flipped Oscar around. Others scrambled to help him hold it still, and my two uncles attacked it with hammers. After a tremendous struggle, we saw that he had a large Mississippi yellow catfish with its head stuck solidly inside an old wooden nail keg. There was no way this beautiful fish could get his head out.

Lester ran to get the dry horseweed stem that we used to measure our biggest fish on. This fish was bigger than the biggest fish we had ever measured before. For many days we feasted on that giant catfish.

The flood lasted for two days. Before the floodwaters started receding, we spent many hours on our front porch watching it. At one point we saw two large wooden covered bridges floating down the high waters about a half-mile to the east. These bridges hit and knocked down huge trees as they rushed by. We watched them break up and drift from our view in this chocolate river and chocolate lake.

The big flood of 1913 did very little damage to our outbuildings, and no damage at all to our livestock barn or to our house. At a very early age I learned the importance of a farmer building on his highest ground and farming the rest.

It wasn't long before a question about floods popped into my gray matter. I ran out to look for Lester so I could ask him. When I finally found him he was swimming in Pipe Creek looking for soft-shelled turtles.

"Lester, do the Indians have any good way to tell when a big flood is coming?"

"They sure do, Little Brother," he said. "When the water in their camp gets up around their knees, they know an awful big flood is on its way!"

| 3 |

CUMMINS 'ROUND THE MOUNTAIN

Mysterious things had happened on our farm during the early timber-clearing days, things that Lester and me learned about only when the folks swapped stories after supper.

One night a man named Walter Cummins was visiting us for supper. He had recently become our tenant farmer and had moved his family into our tenant house. He was helping Dad with the tobacco crops. Dad and Oscar began to tell him about a big man nicknamed "Tug Boat."

Tug Boat, who was from Louisiana, had dragged logs down from the woodlands with his oxen every day until dark. He ate his supper at the end of each day, then always went to his tent to sleep.

One night after midnight Dad and Oscar heard a lot of noise outside. They jumped up and went out to see what was causing the commotion. They saw Tug Boat harnessing up his oxen. Without saying a word, he went up the hill with his oxen and stopped at a large pile of logs. Dad and Oscar followed out to the foot of the hill and watched in the moonlight. When Tug Boat and his oxen went by dragging a big log, they could see he was asleep.

"Don't wake him," Dad warned Oscar.

One at a time, Tug Boat dragged four big logs down the hill to the sawmill. Then the big man unhitched his oxen, fed them, and went back to his tent.

The next morning, Tug Boat denied he had done such a thing, even after Dad and Oscar showed him the logs. Dad could see trouble in his eyes, so he never brought the subject up again. Tug Boat was a very good worker and deserved respect.

"Did Tug Boat ever do any more work for you in his sleep?" Mr. Cummins asked.

"If he did, we never found out about it," said Oscar.

We all worked hard, except Smart Ol' Lester and me, to keep the Hannebaum farm looking like a showplace. The bluegrass pastures and hillsides of the farm always looked well cared for. The big timber on top of the hills was all straight and tall. Dad would cut any timber that wasn't straight. He burned the crooked timber in the cookstove or used it for winter heating.

Walter Cummins had a sly sense of humor and loved to get at Dad about his obsession with clearing out crooked timber.

One morning Mr. Cummins hurried into the house to talk to Mom and Dad. "I heard a mighty strange noise up in your woods last night, John," Mr. Cummins said, sipping from a cup of coffee that Mom handed him. "Did you hear it, too?"

"No, I don't remember any noise last night, except Gussy barking," said Dad.

"This noise lasted so long that I got up and dressed, took the lantern, and went up into your woods to find out what was making all that uproar," said Mr. Cummins.

"Well, that must of been when Gussy was barking," Dad guessed.

"No, I don't reckon so, as I saw your Gussy, and she was just too *scared* to bark," said Mr. Cummins, putting his cup of coffee down and acting out his story in front of Mom and Dad.

"You see, the closer I got to the noise, the louder it got and the scareder I became, and I was so damn scared I couldn't go any further—so I took the lantern bail in my teeth and put my two hands in my own back pockets and started pushing myself forward real hard. Finally I forced myself to get right up next to that racket. Then I scrambled up one of your big trees to keep from getting mauled by that terrible thing thrashing around on the ground. Only then could I make out what it was."

At this point, Mr. Cummins sat down in a chair and mopped his brow silently.

"Well, what was it?" Dad shouted at him.

In a low voice Walter growled, "I quickly shot it twice with my ol' muzzle loader, but I could see it was still moving, so I ran down to your woodshed and got a crosscut saw." He leaned forward, then burst out, *"It was one of your LOGS and it was so damn crooked it couldn't lay still!* As quick as I could I sawed it into four pieces. When I left, those pieces they were still kind of bumblin' into each other, but at least they wasn't making so damn much racket that we couldn't sleep! Now, *that* might of been when your ol' Gussy got up enough courage to bark!" Then Mr. Cummins laughed and hooted because he knew that he had really hooked Dad and pulled him in with his story.

As they got to know Mr. Cummins better, Mom and Dad would break out in laughter at anything and everything he said, even before he finished. They knew there was always another sly joke coming.

| 4 |

DOLLIE, ROCKET, AND PRINCE

Dad loved to tell us about a greyhound he had bought already trained for Dollie when she was eleven years old. I remember seeing the big dog when he was very old and I was very young. His name was Rocket.

Dad knew that Rocket had been trained to wear a harness and to pull a cart. From the moment Dad mentioned it, Dollie wanted Rocket to pull her little red wagon. On her own she tied a light rope from the handle of her wagon to the dog's neck. This harness confused the dog, and because it did not work, frustrated Dollie.

So Dad ordered a fine harness made in a Cincinnati harness shop. He removed the handle from the red wagon and replaced it with two shafts, one to go on each side of the dog.

Dollie made many trips around our spacious lawn in the wagon with Rocket pulling it. Rocket did a fine job, and Dollie was delighted with her precious greyhound and red wagon.

Almost daily Dollie walked two miles round trip up Pipe Creek Road to get the mail for the folks. Soon she began begging Mom and Dad, "*Please* let me take Rocket with the wagon to get the mail this morning, and if he gets tired, I will get out and walk."

"You sound like you think Rocket is able to pull your wagon with you in it on a two-mile trip," said Dad. "Do you think he can make it?"

"Yes, yes, Daddy!" Dollie answered excitedly. "I *know* he can do it. He is so strong."

Dad greased the wheels so the wagon would pull easily, and hitched Rocket to the wagon. He attached a jerk line for Dollie to use to control Rocket.

"I am going along in the buggy," Dad informed her, "to make sure you and Rocket get there and back in the same two pieces."

Rocket always barked when he was excited and happy, and he did a great deal of barking that day. The trip went off without any problems. Dollie rode all the way and Rocket didn't even take a long breath.

Dad made two more trips to our mailbox over the next two days with Dollie and Rocket. The following day, Dad let Dollie and the dog go alone.

They loved going for the mail and were always ready and excited for that wonderful trip.

Dollie and Rocket made many trips on that road with only minor problems. Sometimes on the way home he wanted to run. Sometimes he got into a friendly smelling contest with the other neighborhood dogs. If someone wanted to pass, Dollie would park him off to the side of the road.

Everything went well until one day Bert discovered Rocket lying down at the front gate with only part of the wagon still attached to him. We all knew immediately that something was wrong and that Dollie needed our help.

Well, Rocket hurried along with the family up the road to find Dollie. She was sitting on a big rock about a half mile away, crying her eyes out. She had a lot of cuts and scratches on her.

Bert went on up the road a short distance and through a barbed-wire fence, where he found bits of Dollie's clothes on the wires. He went up the hillside where he found the mail scattered in all directions.

Dollie told us what had happened. "A rabbit ran out in front of Rocket, and he took off like a bolt of lightning after it, right through the barbed-wire fence."

That was where she had been tossed out on her backside, scratched, and cut. She watched Rocket disappear over the ridge, her wagon flying to pieces, and mail falling all over the hillside.

It was a good thing for the rabbit that Mother Nature put a short cotton tail on it instead of a long tail, because Rocket must have been mighty close to it and hungry for a rabbit dinner.

Dollie got a new wagon, but it never did make the trip up Pipe Creek Road behind Rocket to our mailbox again, since rabbits still hopped across the road regularly.

When Dollie was twelve, Dad and Mom gave her a beautiful roan Old Kentucky racehorse named Prince, and she rode him up to the mailbox every day instead.

| 5 |

CLAY MARBLES

When I grew a little older and was able to run after my brothers, one day I discovered a spot of blue clay on the banks of Pipe Creek. A day or so later I found a spot of yellow clay on a nearby hillside. I was delighted with my finds.

Using the colored clay, I could roll up perfectly round little yellow and blue balls. Sometimes I would use half yellow and half blue to make one ball. I took my beautiful work home, and when no one was in the kitchen, I placed my little clay balls all around inside Mom's cookstove oven.

Mom was teaching my sister Dollie how to cook and bake. Dollie was always trying to bake pies or cakes like Mom's famous ones. But this time when she opened the hot oven door to put her pie in, she noticed all the little clay balls on the bottom of the oven. She began to yell my name. She sounded like she wanted to kill me, so I quickly hid out and stayed hid until I thought she had given up the thought of ever seeing me again.

After that I always managed to have a large supply of these clay balls half hidden and baking toward the back of the dark oven. I carried a supply of them in my pockets, and I was very proud of them.

I mainly used them to shoot marbles with. I was good with them and often won the pretty store-bought glass marbles that the neighborhood kids and my brothers used.

My sister, however, never understood. All she was interested in was baking something good to eat in a spotlessly clean oven.

| 6 |

SMOKE-BLOWING MONSTER

One day when I was about five, I was playing all by myself in our fenced-in yard and I was having a wonderful time. Then I began to hear a funny sound, one I had never heard before in all of my short life.

I glanced in the direction of the sound and saw a roaring black hideous monster coming down the road. To make matters worse, it suddenly turned directly into our driveway and roared right toward me. I was never so frightened in all my days! I scrambled away screaming and crying, and dove through the hinged basement window, breaking it. I hid in the potato bin.

My folks had just bought a new black 1915 Maxwell car. I had never seen a car, nor had I ever heard a car motor running. To me, it appeared that the black monster had *eaten* my folks, and I could still see them undigested inside of this monstrosity!

Mom and Dad had hours of explaining to do before they could get me out of the basement. It was three or four days before I would go near that smoke-blowing, roaring creature.

I stood out in the backyard and looked at it for hours. I wondered how it could go without horses hitched to the front of it. Both my Dad's buggy and our fine carriage used horses. Even the school wagon needed horses to pull it.

Oscar tried to get me used to the Maxwell by letting me— or rather *making* me—ride in it while explaining to me how it worked. Oscar must have thought that this was pretty heavy stuff for a five-year-old boy to absorb, but I listened hard. Eventually I got enough of his teachings to become convinced that this four-wheel creature was all right.

Oscar told me how the engine made the wheels go around, and how that made the Maxwell go down the road. He admitted that if the Maxwell got stuck in a mud hole—and there were about thirty of them to every country mile in our neighborhood—you still had to get a horse to pull it out.

One day I heard the garage man say, "This Maxwell's engine is a twenty-five horsepower." I thought awhile and figured that the garage man didn't have much schooling. I knew by looking at the Maxwell that two of our big horses could drag it all over the country, even if the Maxwell was trying to go the other way!

A strange thing began to happen. I had enjoyed many rides in the Maxwell, and now Mom and Dad knew of another place to find me if I didn't show up for dinner. I would be out in the driveway near our big barn, polishing the big brass headlights and other shiny parts of the machine I had come to love, our beautiful Maxwell.

| 7 |

MY FIRST INVENTION

By this time I had heard of inventors. My Uncle Harry Jones had invented a way to keep from losing a large cork if it "blowed out" of our cider barrel. He took the cork and attached it to the barrel with a stout string. It seemed kind of simple, and I figured even I could invent something that easy.

I was already pretty well saturated with the Maxwell. I decided that I would invent something to help me run fast and help me to see in the dark, like this car could.

I spent hours in the tool shop working on my idea. My uncle who had invented the "Cork Keeper"—that was what he called it—told me the rules.

"You will have to keep your invention very secret and not let anyone see you working on it," Harry said solemnly.

After he explained why this was important, I locked myself into the tool shop whenever I worked on my new invention. This was very frustrating for me, since it seemed that all the hired men and all the neighbors were always wanting to get into the tool shop for something. Each time someone wanted to come in I had to put an old gunnysack over my precious invention to hide it.

Dad cut out some very important pieces for it from an old, broken looking glass, and after a few more hours of work, my invention was nearing its "trail run," as I thought my Dad called it. Only later did I learn that the first tryout was called a "trial run." My excitement was growing. Dad, while cutting the mirror glass for me, had seen my invention. He said, "We must keep it a very close secret, and we will do the trial run after dark."

Finally, we both looked over the finished product. It consisted of two pieces. The first part was a contraption that looked like a car's radiator, with front fenders on each side. The second part was like a headlight, and was fixed in the center of the first contraption, because I couldn't find enough parts for a second headlight. Dad said, "It's all right, because some Maxwells only have one headlight since the other one never does work."

Dad and me had quite a tussle getting my invention out the door of the tool shop in total darkness. We made some noise, and ol' Gussy started to bark. We decided we would have to take her along with us to keep her quiet.

Just then we saw the back door of the kitchen open. From inside I heard Mom say loudly, "Oscar, bring me the ten-gauge double barrel." Mom must have figured there were intruders on our place, that they would hear her threat to use the shotgun on them and go home. Dad said, "Don't even breathe for awhile!" By the time Mom finally closed the kitchen door, we had almost run out of courage. I think that was the longest I ever held my breath.

Dad whispered to me, "We will carry your invention up the road past the tobacco barn and stop at the top of the hill by the Old Whirl Hole in Pipe Creek, and then you can try her out by running down the hill."

This *had* to be the right way to do it, because Dad said so. But it was almost another disaster since we both fell down twice in the dark.

The dog ran off up the hillside barking and chasing something. Whatever it was, Gussy put it up a tree and then just stayed there barking. Dad said, "Maybe that's good. Nobody will invade us now, because they will go up on the hill to see what ol' Gussy has treed."

We made it to the top of the hill on the narrow graveled road. Dad helped me get the cardboard fenders and radiator fastened to my shoulders with binder twine. He told me to hold the headlight out in front of me.

The big brass headlights on our Maxwell burned carbide gas, and they had to be lit with a match whenever we wanted to use them. My headlight burned the more commonly used kerosene.

My lamp was made from the bowl of an old kerosene lantern with a still-workable wick in it. I had punched a ring of air intake holes in a circle around the bottom of a square maple syrup can. I had also punched plenty of exhaust holes in its flat top. I had cut a four-inch by six-inch hole in front and covered it with a sliding removable glass lens. Inside the syrup can and to the back I had firmly placed the pieces of looking glass that Dad had cut for me.

Dad struck a match and shielded it from the breeze with his hand while he lit the wick. The headlight really did light up the road! It was summertime, and I could see lots of white millers and other bugs flying toward me.

I ran down the hill. I was thrilled as I picked up speed. As I neared the bottom of the hill, I lost one fender. Then the lens fell out of my headlight, and suddenly the wind from my speed put out the flame.

Instantly I found myself running in total darkness. I ran wildly off the narrow road and collided with a large wooden "No Fishing" sign. The impact totaled my invention.

Lying there in darkness on the ground, dazed and bleeding, I heard ol' Gussy still barking far away, and the sound of my Dad running down the hill toward me.

My first invention was now history, and the lantern parts and the looking-glass reflectors are probably still there somewhere in the weeds.

| 8 |

RESCUE AND DELIVERANCE

My brothers thought it was lots of fun to throw me out into the Whitewater River. Then, before I went under for the last time, they would jump in and rescue me.

I hated this game, but I couldn't run fast enough to get away from them. So out I would be tossed again, and once again they would rescue me.

One day when they did this to me for the fifth time, I swam out of the river by myself before they had a chance to rescue me. Their fun was over. I danced around them and laughed in their faces. That really made them unhappy. Within a few weeks, I was a pretty good swimmer and diver, just like my brothers.

One day we spotted a large old sycamore tree. To get to it, we had to swim across the Whitewater River. The tree had large limbs that hung out over a deep lake of sloppy mud, with no rocks, limbs or any other thing in it.

We soon discovered how much fun it was to climb out on one big smooth limb, wrap our legs around it, hang over this mud lake, and then drop head first into the mud. We found we could sink into mud right up to our ankles, then all the other kids would jump in from the ground level, swim out, and quickly pull the mud-diver out.

The next step was for everyone to jump into the Whitewater River to wash all the mud off. Then it was back up the old sycamore for more thrilling mud-diving, followed by an equal number of rescues performed by the other kids.

We all took many turns at dropping head first from the limb into the mud and then being rescued.

| 9 |

OUT WITH MY FRIENDS

I loved to play with all kinds of animals, and particularly with our farm animals. Every chance I got, I was out with my best friends.

One morning when I was very small and dressed up in fresh clothes, I found my way into the cow lot. We had an old cow named Lil, and she always thought of me as her calf. Lil would lick me so hard that I couldn't stand up.

This morning Lil had me down in the mud, licking me as usual. All of the other cows were standing nearby watching Lil taking care of me when my Mom found me. Mom was really upset and threatened to beat the daylights out of me if I didn't stay out of the cow lot.

A few days later, I tried out the horse lot. The horses started fighting over me and ended up making a circle around me with their heads down.

Oscar spotted me in this circle of horses and rushed in to my rescue. He was also angry with me. He said, "If you don't stay out of the cow lot and the horse lot, I'm going to beat you to one inch of your life!" Just thinking that my hero brother was angry with me was hard on me. Oscar never did paddle me and was always my best friend throughout my life.

But it was the old roosters that gave me the most trouble. If I started out into the barn lot, I first had to stop and look to see where the roosters were, then run for dear life.

My worst problem was going to the outhouse. I could always outrun the roosters to get out there, but when I was finished and wanted to get back to the house, those old roosters would be waiting to do battle at the door. Then they could have their fun!

I would yell for Mom, Dad, Oscar, or anyone to come and help me out. I hated those roosters and never did win a battle with them. I think they must have taken turns standing guard. They knew better than to bother the older folks, but they sure picked on me.

Even if I was just going up into the woods or down on the creek or river or over to sit in the new Maxwell car, the roosters would always spot me and would start in after me. I think I could have been an Olympic runner during my early years because of all the practice they gave me. My need to run faster and faster had helped me think of my first invention—my running contraption.

I loved to be around our pigs and hogs, and we had a lot of them. Oscar raised purebred black Poland China hogs. He kept records on his hogs in leather-bound books, and the books were off limits to us kids. I think he would have killed us if we messed with those books.

Oscar went to Iowa from time to time to buy top-of-the-line hogs for breeding with his other top-of-the-line hogs. He was very proud of these purebred animals, and he even entered one of them in the World's Fair in London. This hog took top honors as the world's heaviest hog at nine months and thirteen days. Oscar always raised the largest and heaviest hogs around.

Talk about shipping a purebred hog to London caused a lot of excitement, since there wasn't anyone in our area who had been more than a few hundred miles away from home.

Oscar's hogs were taller than the hog pens. I often saw them looking over the top panels of their pens when it came time for feeding.

Oscar put me on top of his purebred hogs and I rode them like horses. Then he took pictures of me riding them around. I really loved all the attention that I received from Oscar and from these black-and-white pictures.

One day, Oscar placed me on top of a hog he was planning to ship to the World's Fair in Chicago, Illinois. It was named Orange B and it took top honors for being the world's biggest and longest hog at the fair that year. This was the type of hog that was needed for lard and meat in the early 1900s.

I enjoyed resting on top of the sows when they were lying down and nursing their little pigs. I loved to stick my fingers down where the little pigs were nursing. Sometimes one of the little pigs would make a mistake and grab onto my fingers and suck. It didn't take long, however, before they decided my finger wasn't one of their "dinner plates" and made me laugh by spitting it out.

Once Gussy had puppies. When they were big enough to wean, the folks gave her puppies away to the neighbors, and then they gave Gussy three baby pigs to raise because one old sow had three too many in her litter to feed. Gussy let these three little pigs nurse until they were ready to wean. They turned out to be very fat little pigs, but to my disappointment, they never did learn to bark.

|10|

LAND TURTLES AND SORE FINGERS

On top of a wooded ridge a mile or so from our house was a place known as Bear Wallow. It was fed by springs and was supposed to be where the black and brown bears cooled off during the summer months in the early days.

When me and Lester spotted Bear Wallow for the first time, we had to explore it. We found no bears, but we did find hundreds of land turtles under the banks of a shallow pool of water.

We decided to put dozens of turtles on their backs around the grassy banks of the pool to keep them from leaving. I had to work fast to keep up with Lester, and I got careless. One big turtle got three of my fingers on my right hand between his upper and lower shell and clamped down on them.

The pain drove me into a fit. I hollered for Lester to help me. Lester said, "There is no way to get you loose from that turtle now, but he will let you go at *sundown*, and that is in about four hours or so."

I howled, "It hurts awful! I can't wait that long! It's almost suppertime, and I can't eat left-handed!"

Smart Ol' Lester thought for a minute, then found two big rocks and placed the biggest one on the grassy bank. Then he said, "Put the turtle on the rock." With my eyes shut tight, I asked, "What are you going to do with that other big rock in your hand?"

Lester didn't answer. He just said, "Hold still." Down came the large rock in his hand with all of his might, smashing the poor turtle's shell to smithereens. I couldn't even recognize my three fingers.

For a week or so, my fingers were very sore and so was my rear end. I didn't see Lester for three days, but I could hear him in an upstairs bedroom howling about his sore rear end. Lester was not allowed to come out, except with an escort.

I overheard Dad telling Mom, "Those darn kids are going to drive us crazy." Later I asked Mom what he meant, and Mom said, "That means you kids are a lot of trouble, but we really love you all."

|11|

THE WHITE WORM PATCH

One summer morning when I was nearly six and Lester was eight, we were out with Gussy crossing over a new pasture to bring the cows home. Dad had created the meadow from timberland that he had cleared of all trees and then seeded with bluegrass.

We discovered a new path over a small rise and followed it through some of Dad's choice sugar maple, red oak, and ash trees. We thought we might be able to get the cows back from the new pasture using this shortcut.

Suddenly we noticed a brilliant white spot on the ground ahead of us. Never in our short lives had we seen anything like it. Lester said, "Dad must have spilled an awful lot of that cow salt."

"Do you think we should tell Dad about it?" I asked.

Lester thought it over very heavily, then said, "No, if Dad

had lost that much weight, he would be awful light-footed, know that he had lost something, and would then look to see what it was. If he did it, he already knows."

I stopped Lester in his tracks, and said, "Lester, you are the smartest man I ever saw!" In my eyes, he was already a man.

Lester casually spat some farm tobacco toward a rock and said, "Well, one of us has to think."

We cautiously approached the white stuff and found that it wasn't salt after all. It looked like a million big, round dead worms. We got a long stick and poked them, but they didn't move any, so we rolled some of them around.

Me and Lester were a little scared of being bitten by these millions of worm-like things. Our experience with the land turtles at Bear Wallow was still fresh in our minds. I told Lester, "You've got to think of something we can do to gather some and take them to the house to show Mom and Dad."

Lester sat down on a half-rotten stump. After awhile he said, "I just got a lot of thinking done and I am tired, so now *you* do some thinking."

I was surprised and said, "I guess I never done much thinking before."

"Why not?" Lester asked.

"I guess it is because I am always busy doing something else," I answered.

But as I spoke, a plan began to form in my mind. I began to figure out how to tell if those white worms could bite us or hurt us.

We needed our faithful dog Gussy for my plan, and I could hear her barking somewhere over the brow of the hill. I went to find her and came out on higher ground than Gussy.

I could see out over a large area of land. Gussy was down there chasing two rabbits, and I could tell she thought she was chasing only one rabbit. I couldn't believe our old dog was so dumb.

Then I thought, "Well, I guess she is pretty dumb or she wouldn't of let those three little pigs nurse on her until they were nearly at the hog stage of life."

I stood there for a short while and watched those two

smart ol' rabbits while they pulled the old relay trick on my dog. The first rabbit would rest while the second rabbit would get chased. Then the second rabbit would rest behind a bush while the other one would dash around in plain sight.

I hated it that these rabbits were smarter than my dog. I called for her to come to me. Tired ol' Gussy came right away, and we went back to where Lester was resting from all of his thinking near the patch of mysterious worm-like things.

"Whatcha gonna do with Gussy?" Lester inquired from his stump.

Proudly I revealed my plan: "Lester, you get on the other end of that patch of worms, and I will hold Gussy on this end. You call her and I will turn her loose. If she runs through the worms without yelping, why, then maybe they don't bite. Then we can put some of them in our pockets and take them to the house."

Well, we did all that and Gussy was not bitten. We closely examined those funny white things, but we still didn't know what they were.

When we got back to the house, thrilled with our new discovery, Dad wanted to see what we had. He examined our worms, then said, "You kids must have found that old petrified ringworm bed up by the new pasture." Walter Cummins, our tenant tobacco grower, agreed.

"Where did these worms come from?" I wanted to know.

"These worms," said Dad, "along with thousands of other very large and very small creatures, roamed this planet millions of years ago and are now extinct. Or in plain language for you two kids, they are gone forever from this Earth."

Dad added, "These tiny creatures are petrified in their original likeness forever—if they are never disturbed. Now you two kids, carefully take all you have in your pockets back and put them where you found them." Even at that time, our Dad was very concerned about protecting all creatures, even those now extinct or those nearing extinction.

I overheard Walter Cummins tell Dad that there were some mighty funny creatures on this farm and that some of them should be kept in cages. They both laughed, and I knew they were talking about Lester and me.

|12|

MRS. MILBOURNE AND MR. KOONCE

About this time, I began to notice an older lady working around our house. She always seemed to be very busy. One day I saw Mom talking to her, so later I asked Mom, "Who is that old lady?"

Mom was very stern with me and said, "You must always call her 'Mrs. Milbourne.' She may be here for a long time and you kids must treat her with great respect."

I had heard a new word. I asked Mom, "What does *respect* mean?"

"It means that you and Lester and all others of this house must treat her very nicely at all times. Mrs. Milbourne is our housekeeper and cook, and she will help all of us by helping your Mom," she explained.

As time went on, Mrs. Milbourne became more acquainted with our house, with our summer kitchen, and with us kids. We grew to respect her, and more than that, to love her.

Our summer kitchen was actually another house about fifty feet from our big house. The summer kitchen had an attached smokehouse for preserving all kinds of meats. Meat could not be kept very long without sugar-curing and heavy smoking because we had no refrigerators in those days. Large fish, chickens, ducks, beef, pork, and sausages went through the sugar-curing and smoking process.

The summer kitchen had two rooms, a large, fully equipped kitchen and an even larger dining room. Both were used heavily during the harvesting of our tobacco crop and again during the grading and curing of the tobacco during the winter months.

About twenty-five men helped us during this harvest cycle. Dad said many times, "If you grow tobacco, you never get done working with it. It always takes thirteen months or more for the complete cycle of a tobacco crop."

I liked to be around tobacco, to smell it and to listen to

the tobacco men tell their tall stories. Boy, did I learn things from them! I didn't know words could be dirty or bad, and when something slipped out, Mom would always whip me. After she used that leather strap on me she would always say, "Why didn't you *ask* me if you didn't know what that word meant?" It took me, and even sharp Ol' Lester, a long time to conquer the misunderstanding of what to say and what not to say.

Poor Mrs. Milbourne. At first she worked way too hard, I guess, because she was afraid of losing her job. My Mom was good to her and said, "You are working too hard, and from now on, you are only to work when I tell you to." This made Mrs. Milbourne very happy. Now she could take a nap in the afternoon and be rested for getting our supper.

My folks also had a chore man who worked for them, Mr. Koonce. He did chores such as feeding the horses, cows, chickens, and some of the hogs. Dad owned all of the farm, the crops taken from it, and all of the non-registered animals. Oscar owned all of the purebred and registered animals and he fed them all, since that feed had to be carefully mixed, measured, and weighed, with accurate records kept on each of these special animals.

Mom laid down the law about the chore man's name, too. "You kids don't call him anything else, only 'Mr. Koonce.'"

Mr. Koonce never had much to say, but he always did his work well and on time. After that he would just sit around anywhere and stare at the ground or at the nearby hill or just into space.

I overheard Dad say to Mom, "That poor old fellow must have deep problems, but he doesn't want to take his problems to anyone else."

As time went on we all got used to Mr. Koonce and his quiet ways, and we thought it was probably just his way of relaxing. Dad told him, so I heard Mom say, that if he ever had any complaints or didn't feel good, that Dad would listen and get help for him.

Mr. Koonce had a nice room upstairs in our house. It had a large easy chair, a water basin, dresser, chest of drawers, clothes closet, bed, and other items for comfort.

Right to the minute every morning, Mr. Koonce would come downstairs for his breakfast. Mrs. Milbourne would always say, "Good morning, Mr. Koonce. You will never have to starve or cook for yourself because you are always right on time." She bustled around, then added, "Why, I could set my clock by you, and it would always be right on."

Mr. Koonce was good to us kids and to our farm animals, and we grew to like him very much. He always stayed to himself with any of his deep-seated problems. These problems, however, started to have an effect on his eating habits. At times he would refuse to eat anything, but he always did the chores on time.

At this point, Mom, being a trained nurse, tried to get him to go with her to see the family doctor at Brookville, Indiana, the seat of Franklin County. Mr. Koonce refused and said he would get better.

A few days later, the old fellow didn't come downstairs for his breakfast. Oscar said, "I will go and knock on his door." When there was no answer, Oscar opened the door, quickly closed it, and went back down the stairs to the kitchen, where we all ate.

Mom quickly noticed by the look on Oscar's face that something was wrong. When breakfast was finished, she asked, "Is Mr. Koonce sick?"

Without answering Mom's question, Oscar said, "Put the kids outside." This was done. Me and Lester didn't really understand what had happened to Mr. Koonce, and our folks wanted it that way. We took off running for the Whirl Hole to check out what animals had left their tracks in the sand during the night.

That afternoon we saw a beautiful shiny black wagon pulled by a team of black horses coming down the road. It was hard for Lester and me to understand how the wagon could roll along so quietly on the dirt and gravel road. Since we were wet from swimming we hid in a big patch of tall weeds between Pipe Creek and the dirt road to watch.

The beautiful wagon was long and narrow with both sides fitted with long windows. A tall man all dressed in black sat in an open-air seat, just like the driver on a stagecoach. Two buggies with fringe around their tops followed closely behind the fancy black wagon.

The procession stopped at our front gate. We saw six men, all dressed in black, climb down from the buggies. Quietly they opened the back door of the black wagon, pulled a long, shiny box from it, and carried it into our house. The tall driver remained silently in place with the reins held in his hands.

Me and Lester were so scared by this strange and mysterious happening at our place that we didn't say a word, not even a whisper.

In just a few minutes all six men came out of our house carrying the long shiny box between them, followed quietly by Mom, Dad, Oscar, Mrs. Milbourne, Bert, and Dollie. The strangers placed the large box back into the fancy carriage. We could look through the windows and see the box sitting on royal blue velvet inside.

We hid until the little procession quietly disappeared back down the road. Then we saw that Dad was sitting out on the porch by himself, smoking his pipe. We raced each other to get to his side because we both had a jillion questions to ask him.

That afternoon we had a long discussion with our Dad using strange words like *death, coffin* or *casket, burial, funeral,* and *hearse,* or the ceremonial *caisson* for very important people like kings or presidents. We even discussed why a burial ground was called a cemetery in town and a graveyard out in the country.

"How could the hearse not make any noise as it was being pulled down the road?" I asked.

"So you noticed that, too, eh?" Dad said, smiling. "The undertaker told me it is a new invention, medium-soft India rubber tread about one-inch square, fastened around the rims of the wooden-spoke wheels. Plus the wagon already has soft springs under each wheel. It is a sign of respect for the departed."

Only Mom, Dad, Oscar, and Mrs. Milbourne got to go to the funeral for Mr. Koonce. Later I heard the folks talking about Albert Koonce being at the burial. They said he was probably Mr. Koonce's only son.

Me and Lester missed Mr. Koonce for a long time. When-

ever we mentioned his name we spoke quietly out of respect.
We never did find out what his deep-seated problems were.

|13|

TOBACCO

Lester and me saw nothing wrong with tobacco and even
learned how to smoke and chew it from watching the men. We
also learned how to make cigars and plug tobacco.

However, if Mom caught us smoking or chewing, she
would tan our hides. And if our brother Bert ever caught us
smoking, he would always tell Mom.

In later years I quit using any kind of tobacco since it is
such a dirty habit. In the early days, however, no one was aware
that tobacco caused any health problems, so I used it along
with everyone else.

Tobacco was a tedious crop to grow in those early days. It
needed lots of care. Dad and Mom would always sow the tiny
little seeds in a twelve-foot by fifty-foot "hot bed." This bed of
dirt was kept covered by cheesecloth fastened to a pole that
ran all the way around the hot bed. This served to hold the
cheesecloth up off the tiny new tobacco plants. The tobacco
seeds were so tiny that a teaspoon full would grow enough
plants, if my memory serves me right, for five or six acres.

When the plants were four to five inches across and the
frost danger was over and it was raining, the plants were trans-
planted. No matter how hard it was raining, the plants were
hurriedly removed from the hot bed and planted in rows four
to five feet across in the field.

Our family grew the Beach Burley and the Stand-up Burley varieties. These were both large types of tobacco plants.

Many men, women, and even kids were used in the field,
because the transplanting had to be completed before the rain
stopped and while the ground was still muddy. Otherwise, some
of the plants would die.

During tobacco's long growing time, all the weeds had to be hoed out, and all the sprouts or "suckers" had to be pulled off. The tops had to be cut away so the plant would make larger leaves and to keep it from going to seed. The large tobacco worms had to be handpicked off the leaves.

Then, after all of this, we would pray for summer rains.

|14|

TOBACCO WORMS

WARNING: A tobacco worm is a large green monster of a worm with beady eyes and a grinder-like mouth! Their mouths look like the business end of a rock crusher. Each worm has two rows of stout hairy legs that all walk in the same direction. At their rear end there is a very large horn that sticks straight up, and the worm uses this big horn to honk with when another worm won't move over. These big green tobacco worms make a chattering sound, and it is this sound that makes it easy to find them on the tobacco plant.

Tobacco worms eat tobacco and develop a ravenous appetite for it. This is why some tobacco farmers have lost their entire crops to them. In my opinion, the tobacco user should quit competing with those large, green, very determined worms.

When me and Lester had to pick the big green worms from the tobacco plants for the first time, we didn't know what to do with them. The tobacco plants were larger than we were and nobody could see us to teach or correct us.

We decided to put the worms into our large pockets. Pretty soon Lester said, "My pockets are all full of worms."

I said, "Mine are, too."

"We will have to kill them," I said, "or they will get back onto the tobacco plants. You're the smartest—how do we kill them?"

Just then Lester yelled, "*Ouch!* I just tried to get one out of my pocket and it bit me! Don't put your fingers into your pockets, as it really hurts when they bite you."

We stood there for awhile, squirming and feeling sorry for ourselves.

Finally Smart Ol' Lester got an idea. "I know! Let's run down between the tobacco rows to that deep hole in Pipe Creek and drown them with our pants on."

I didn't quite understand, but I was willing to try anything.

Lester tried to explain as we ran. "Don't you see? They'll be dead then and can't bite our fingers when we pull them out of our pockets!"

We had a great time trying to out-dog-paddle Gussy. We had such a good time swimming that we forgot we were there to drown the large, mean tobacco worms in our pockets.

Brother Bert showed up and started hollering at us to go home. We were afraid of Bert because he often tried to beat us up, or he would tell Mom what we were doing and make it sound awful. We swam out on the other side of Pipe Creek and ran off up the hill to the woods where we could hide until suppertime.

When we got to the house that evening, we washed our hands as usual and went to stand by the dining room table. Everyone had to stand at the side of their chairs until Dad sat down. Then all eight of us, including Mrs. Milbourne, could sit and start eating.

Lester had a lifelong habit of putting his hands in his pockets when he was around the house so he would look very important.

When Dad sat down that night, Lester pulled his hands from his pockets, and started to sit down. He looked at his hands and turned pale. His fingers were shiny and covered with green worm skins. Mom gasped, "Lester, what is that on your hands?"

Lester didn't say anything and tried to hide his hands. Mom grabbed him and hurried him off to his bedroom. There she made him wash his hands again in the wash basin. To my surprise, Mom came back to the table without Lester.

We all ate our supper, but I had lost my appetite. I remem-

bered that my pockets were also full of drowned green tobacco worms.

Poor Ol' Lester. He had to eat all alone later, and I didn't
feel so good myself.

|15|

THINGS ARE HUMMING

When the big tobacco leaves started to turn a yellowish gold-
en-brown color, the whole plant was ready to cut at ground
level. The workers split each tobacco stalk from the top to nearly
the bottom of the big end. The tobacco was then placed astrad-
dle of oak sticks about five feet long, and the loads were then
hauled immediately on wagons to one of our four big tobacco
curing barns.

All over the inside of each barn, from the roof to ground
level, tobacco was hung in crowded rows. There it stayed for a
few weeks until it turned a deep golden brown.

Then a lot of men with know-how came to our barns and
worked in grading rooms in one corner of each barn. Large
heating stoves in the grading rooms kept the men warm during the winter months. In something like an assembly line,
these men stripped all of the leaves from the tobacco stalks.
The first man took off the bottom four or five leaves and placed
them in a neat pile. The second man took off the next five or
six leaves, starting from where the first man left off. He placed
his leaves in a neat pile, then passed the stalk down the line to
the next man. The third man took off the next four or five, and
added them to his pile. This continued until all the leaves were
removed and graded into five piles.

Each pile was a different grade of tobacco, starting with
what was called Trash, then Luggs, followed by Bright Leaf,
and Red Leaf. The last pile was called Tops.

One of the men would then take fourteen to sixteen leaves
from the pile called Trash, and, using one of the other Trash

leaves, tie them into a "hand" of tobacco. Each hand was neatly stacked.

This was done with each grade of tobacco. It was very important that each hand of tobacco was kept in its own grade. All of the tobacco grading and handling was done in damp, rainy weather, so the leaves wouldn't break up.

When the lowest-hanging unsorted tobacco stalks were removed and graded, it freed up space for the graded hands of tobacco. They were quickly returned from the grading room and placed in stacks or "bulks" in the five grade orders. These bulks grew wider and taller as more tobacco was returned from the grading room.

This process was called "bulking it down" for the so-called "June sweat." If the men did a good job on a bulk of tobacco so that it was solid with few or no air pockets, the tobacco would hold its case, color, and aroma for a long time without going moldy. If all the steps were done in a good tobacco barn with adjustable ventilation, the tobacco would be top grade.

The tobacco was allowed to stay in bulk for as long as necessary. A prospective buyer could pull out a sample hand of tobacco and examine it for good color and good aroma. If the leaves had any holes or tears in them, they were used for cigar fillers, then wrapped with first-grade leaf to make a fine-looking cigar.

When my folks were ready to sell their tobacco and the price was good, they would contact three or four of the largest tobacco processing companies and let them know how many tons they had for sale.

Dad had a twenty-one-foot-long platform scale in the entrance to one of our barns. All of the tobacco and livestock were weighed right to the pound. This way, Dad knew exactly how much each buyer took.

Dad contacted the auctioneers and scheduled a day for them to be at our place. Then he contacted the company representatives again, inviting them to bid against each other for a whole bulk or a fraction of a bulk.

When the auctioneers started the bidding they created a lot of excitement in the big tobacco barns. Us kids would laugh at all that funny auctioneer talk. Usually about a dozen kids could be found standing around with their parents. We took turns standing on a wooden box to play "auctioneer." I wasn't very good at it, but my brother Bert got to be pretty good.

The real auctioneer would shorten his chant by using words like this: "quata quata" meant twenty-five cents, "hah hah" meant fifty cents, and "ree ree" meant seventy-five cents.

Bert would stand on the box and launch into it:

"Step right up folks! Take a good look at that beautiful bale of tobacco hands. Now who'll give me a quata quata, a quata quata, come on, let's hear a quata . . . Yep, I gotta *quata.*

"Now who'll give me a hah hah? Take a good look folks and who'll give me a hah hah, a hah hah, a hah hah . . . Yep, I gotta *hah hah.*

"Now I gotta hah hah—now I need a ree ree. Who'll give me a ree ree for that ex-ceptional bale? Come on folks let's hear a ree ree, do I hear a ree ree? I *got* a hah hah—who'll raise that? Going once, going twice, come on folks, check out that rich color and aroma, take a good look. Do I hear a ree ree? GONE for a *hah hah.* Sold to the man with a fine hand of tobacco in his left hand—Reynolds Tobacco Company." Auction tobacco was always sold to a tobacco company, never to an individual.

As the word got around, sometimes there would be more tobacco company representatives than we had planned on. My Dad found this was a good way to sell tobacco. With no set price involved the sale always went to the highest bidder.

The average grower in the Indiana hill country would have an acre or two of tobacco. My folks grew forty to forty-five acres each year. Our four large tobacco barns were nearly always full after harvest.

After the valuable leaves were stripped from the tobacco stalks in the grading room, the remaining stalks were tossed in a mammoth pile outside. The pile was half as large as the barn itself. Later, when our pond froze over in the winter, we would haul tobacco stalks to the pond by horse-drawn sleigh to burn at ice-skating parties.

At the pond the stalks were separated into four or five large piles, and one of them was set on fire each time we had a big skating party. The flames were twenty feet high and blue hot. The tobacco stalk bonfires caused lots of excitement and enjoyment.

Dad had recently hired a Mr. Gardener from Cincinnati, Ohio. Mr. Gardener was Dad's foreman for the wintertime tobacco processing in the big curing barns. He had contracted what was called "infantile paralysis"—polio. He was a small man who did most of his moving around in a bent-over posture.

By profession Mr. Gardener had been an ice-skating instructor in Cincinnati. The ice gave him the freedom to move with great ease, and he seemed to be able to do all the tricks known by man on ice skates.

He explained, "I was told by someone to take a much-needed vacation from skating instruction, and this is how I wanted to do it."

Mr. Gardener often put on an ice-skating show, and all of the neighborhood kids were amazed at his abilities. Afterwards he gave lessons to all of us.

It wasn't long until the folks bought a brand new tobacco-plant-setting machine. This was a new invention, and a crowd of people came to our place to watch the machine working. This made it much easier to set out the forty acres or more of young tobacco plants each year.

The tobacco-setting machine could also be used to set out all kinds of other small plants. Even with this, we still employed a lot of men, and things were really humming around the Hannebaum farm.

I really felt sorry for Mom and Mrs. Milbourne. They had to work hard to feed all of these men who were planting, harvesting, and grading or bulking down the tobacco. They would butcher six or seven chickens, peel twenty pounds of potatoes, and bake a dozen loaves of bread at one time, not to mention baking an endless supply of wonderful pies and cakes. The cooking and handwork were amazing. The heat from the wood-burning cookstove that they had to work around was ferocious.

When Dad asked Mom about getting some more kitchen help, Mom would always say, "They would only be in our way."

|16|

UNCLE HARRY'S UNDERWATER INVENTION

Lester and me were just a frog's eyelash away from drifting off to sleep late one mid-summer night. We were just waiting for a kiss from Mom and a hug from Dad. Suddenly we heard someone knock at our door, followed by roars of laughter coming from our parlor room. Instantly we sneaked out of our beds, slipped down the stairs, and hid behind a big easy chair in the parlor to watch the fun.

Our Uncle Harry Jones had come to visit!

"Did you ride your horse or walk tonight, Harry?" Dad asked.

"I am out horsing around this beautiful moonlit evening, John," Harry said, grinning. "I was several miles up the road when I caught the distinct smell of one of Flora's famous pies cooling out in your summer kitchen." Mom loved to feed pie or cake to her brothers when they stopped by.

"Not long ago, you and Bob *rowed* your way down our road looking for pie. Too bad you can't do that except when it floods," Dad said, as Mom placed a warm berry pie on a side table.

"I would be willing to *swim* over for pie as good as this," Harry replied, inhaling the delicious smell. "Of course, there was a time when I was deathly afraid of swimming, but that was when I was still just a tyke in diapers."

"How did you get over that fear, Harry, since you are now such a fine swimmer?" Dad asked, before taking a bite of Mom's pie. Me and Lester sat there smelling that mouth-watering pie, but didn't dare give ourselves away.

"Well, let me tell you about one afternoon when I ended up on the wrong side of Pipe Creek," Harry said, sitting down in an easy chair. Mom handed him a huge piece of pie on one of her best china plates. Lester and me rolled our ears out and leaned a little away from our hiding place so we wouldn't miss a word.

"I was a little tyke down on Pipe Creek fishing, and after awhile I figured out that I must be standing near an ant hill."

"Why, Brother Dear, did you get ants in your pants?" Mom asked, giggling. Me and Lester thought we might die trying to keep from laughing out loud.

"Yes, as a matter of fact, I did," Uncle Harry admitted. "I quickly removed my pants and tried to shake out every last one of them damn ants. All afternoon that lazy dog of mine had done nothing—only snap at gnats and sleep—but when I waved my pants . . . " Harry shook his head sadly. Mom and Dad were helpless with laughter. "You guessed it, he grabbed my short pants and swam right across Pipe Creek with them."

"Well, Brother," Mom said between her giggles, "maybe your dog was just trying to help you out. Maybe she was trying to drown those ants for you, like Lester and Harold tried to drown tobacco worms in their pants!"

Me and Lester sobered up and looked at each other, hoping hard that Mom hadn't spotted us. But nothing happened, so we figured we were still safely hidden.

It was easy to tell that Uncle Harry was now reliving that bad experience. He sputtered in an indignant voice, "Well, how would you like to be a little kid in your birthday suit, with your lazy ol' dog laying on the other side of the deep creek with your pants, laughing its fool head off at you?"

"Oh, it wasn't all *that* bad, was it, Harry?" said Mom, snickering. "You still had your diapers on, didn't you?"

"No," replied Uncle Harry, "they had ants in them, too, and I had pulled them off with my short pants. When my dog was about halfway across, they drifted out and floated on down Pipe Creek."

Lester whispered into my left eyeball, "Yeah, and I'll bet his ol' dog always got its breath in short pants!" I was already in a hilarious state, and Lester's pun almost turned me into duck-puddle soup.

"For the life of me," Uncle Harry continued loudly, "I couldn't get that dog to bring my clothes back. I threw a stick across Pipe Creek near my pants and hollered, 'Fetch!' My dog would bring the stick back every time I threw it across the creek, but I could never make her understand to bring back my pants instead of the stick."

"Well, Harry, maybe those pants were just too distasteful for any smart dog to put its mouth on after it once got a taste of them," Mom said, still having fun with her brother.

"Yes folks, all that ol' dog could do was sit on the other side, yapping, snapping at gnats, and wagging its tail in the dry sand, scattering it all over my wet clothes."

"Well, Harry, how *did* you get your pants back?" asked Mom. "I see you're wearing them now!" She broke out in giggles again.

Uncle Harry moved his easy chair close to Dad, now with his back toward Mom. "I knew I was too bashful to walk all the way home nude from the waist down, and I knew I couldn't get my clothes by swimming over and back, since I didn't know how to swim, so I had to invent a way to get my pants myself."

Me and Lester were now leaning way out on both sides of the easy chair so we could hear more about "inventing," our favorite word.

Dad also leaned over closer to Uncle Harry. "Yep, necessity is the mother of inventions," he said quietly. "What did you invent that day, Harry?"

"First, I pulled off my shirt, and carefully buried it in the sand. I didn't want my dog to get its mouth on that, too.

"About that time, by accident I stubbed my big toe on a rock on the edge of the creek bank. I had to sit down to nurse my achy toe while tears ran down my cheeks. While I was sitting there cussing that big rock, my ingenuity somehow clicked into high gear.

"I picked up that heavy rock and another one about the same weight. Carrying one in each hand, I held my breath and walked down into the water. I decided I would try to keep walking as fast as I could across the bottom of that deep ol' creek. John, my heart was pounding so loud with fear that I knew I would probably never take a bath again, and probably faint at the sound of rain on the roof—if I ever made it over and back without drowning." He paused to eat more pie.

Me and Lester slowly put our heads together, and Lester

whispered, "I guess that's why Uncle Harry doesn't wash his face and hair very often." I nodded my head in agreement, and added, "And his socks, too." I held my nose and we struggled to keep quiet as we giggled.

We could hear Uncle Harry's booming voice again, so once more we eased out slightly from behind each side of the easy chair.

"As I started in, the water quickly came up to my hips and then to my armpits. Now the water was up to my neck and I had only gone three or four steps. I took in a lot more wind and closed my eyeballs just before the water came over the top of my head. I went deeper and faster."

He paused to make sure Mom was listening, then rumbled on. "Suddenly something pecked me under my armpit—that made my eyes pop open! Then another peck hit me right along my belly button, nearly causing me to drop my rocks!

"I realized now that I could *see* underwater if I opened my eyes, so I looked around and spotted a big bass aiming right for my nose! I wiggled my head and scared him off, but he got in several more pecks on my body and legs. I couldn't drop my rocks to defend myself, and that ol' bass was definitely determined to get me by the nose!

"By now I was just plain out of air, and my lungs were hurting something awful. I thought to myself, 'If I had walked home without my pants, at least I would be alive and not drowned.'

"But with the very next step I took, my nose popped up out of the water, and I saw that the other bank was only five or six feet away. I had made it!"

Mom hadn't taken one bite of her pie because she was giggling out of control. When she got her breath, she asked, "Did you check all of your personal parts, Brother Dear, to see if any was missing? And is that why you are still a bachelor?"

That did it for Lester and me. We could no longer hold in our laughter. That night I learned for sure that a kid could really die from laughing too hard. I held my sides and rolled around on the floor trying to get air into my lungs, and so did Lester.

Mom and Dad jumped up and grabbed us, laughing too hard to be angry, but they were clearly upset that we had listened in. We were sent to bed without our nightly kiss from her and our hug from him. At the time I couldn't understand why they were so upset with us. Later I realized they were probably afraid we would follow in our Uncle Harry's dangerous footsteps.

In bed I whispered, "Lester, isn't it funny how ants love to be on uncles?" Lester laughed, but after a short silence he said, "Tomorrow, we'll have to try walking on the bottom of Pipe Creek, just like Uncle Harry did!"

"Yep," I agreed. "I was just thinking the same thing, but I am going to keep my clothes on when I try it!"

"So am I," Lester replied.

The very next afternoon, me and Lester slipped away and followed Pipe Creek to where it joined the deep Whitewater River. We each found two large rocks, one for each hand. We were both surprised at how well Uncle Harry's invention worked—it was so easy that there was nothing to it!

Several days later, me and Lester were down at Pipe Creek cutting horseweed stems. We used them for measuring anything we got into an argument over, and we also liked the dried-up stems because they were completely hollow. With both ends cut off, they can be used for drinking straws or to blow paper spit-balls.

"I just had a great idea, Harold," Lester said, looking into one of the stems and seeing daylight at the other end.

"Okay," I said, "shoot!" It was always exciting to me when Lester was willing to let me in on one of his great ideas.

"Now listen real close, Little Brother. When we go down into the real deep water, like in the Whitewater River, or in the deep ponds in Pipe Creek, if we could use these hollow horseweed stems to breathe through, we could stay underwater for a longer time!"

I jumped to my feet and grabbed one. I cut off the other end and sucked air down through it. He did the same thing.

"Come on!" he yelled. "It works real good! Now just remember, dummy, to suck the air down through it, and blow the used air out of your big nose!"

We filled the big pockets of our overalls with rocks, so our hands could be free to hold the horseweed stems straight up from our mouths. Last year's dried-out stems were light, long and easy to hold onto. They stuck up far above the water's surface.

We practiced our breathing before we got in too deep. It was easy to learn, and soon we went way under.

Down in the deep water, we loved to watch the big funny bass, the even bigger catfish, and the little molly hogs, all staring peacefully back at us as they circled through wiggly sunbeams that slanted down through the crystal-clear waters.

I don't know how long we were under with the fishes, but that day we had one of the best times of our young lives.

After we surfaced, I pointed back down to the water and said, "Les, did you see that big hungry bass swimming our way, chasing that luscious fat minnow?"

"Ya, ah deed," replied Les, sounding awful funny. I quickly looked around at him and saw he still had the horseweed stem in his mouth. He pulled it out and said, "Yes, I saw that big bass. Whatcha think I was down there for, to watch you blow bubbles out of your big ugly nose?" I pushed my nose up with my finger to make it as ugly for him as possible.

"Why," I asked with my nose still pushed up, "do the bass turn the little minnows around so they swallow them head first?" Lester didn't reply right away, so I added, "If you don't know, maybe we should ask Dad."

"Naw," my brother drawled. "Dad would just spend hours talking about how he and George Shebler always land such big bass fish using little minnows. I know the answer, Little Brother. The reason they always turn the luscious minnow around in their big ugly mouth is because they are awful tender-hearted fish, and they want the little minnow to think he can swim on through because he can see the light at the far end of their stomach."

Well, I almost bought his answer. But then he outrageously continued, "Some of the larger bass even have something like a mirror inside at their far end. That way, the minnow can see himself and leave, thinking he is already there!"

I tried to push him back into the deep water, but couldn't.

Finally we sat down together in the hot sand to get warm.

"The *real* reason they always turn the luscious minnow around, Little Brother," said Lester, "is that a bass won't swallow a minnow tail first because everything on the minnow is slanting the wrong way."

Thinking deeply about this problem for the first time, I replied, "Kind of like streamlining him, huh? That means he must switch the luscious minnow end for end, or the minnow could get hung up on something inside his throat."

"That's right, Harold. Now you've *finally* got the right idea."

I thought hard on it for a few minutes. "So maybe, Lester, this is why a bass will not go for luscious live minnow bait if it is tied to the fishing line going forwards. Do you think maybe the fishermen should turn their minnows around to swim backwards, to save the big bass the trouble?"

"Maybe we should string you on a line going backwards, Little Brother," replied Lester lazily, almost asleep in his warm sand bed. "Then you will see how much fun it is to be backwards bass bait!"

As the summer went by, we learned to keep hoards of dried-up hollow stems, cleanly cut off at both ends, scattered along Pipe Creek and the Whitewater River. Then whenever we needed to hide from Bert or Mom, we could grab one and disappear like Navy frogmen. We usually didn't do it when we saw Dad coming, however, because we knew we were seldom in any kind of serious trouble with him.

|17|

A GIFT FOR DAD

One hot Indian-summer day I was listening to Mom while she talked on the telephone to a neighbor. Mom said, "I will have to get John something because he will soon be forty-five years old."

That scared me somehow, and I ran to find Lester. He was up to his knees in the mud behind our livestock barn. He said, "Help me, Harold, I can't get out!"

"But if I get into that mud to help you," I said, "I'll just get stuck, too."

Lester thought for awhile, and then said, "I believe I will try to do what Walter Cummins done to get closer to that crooked log."

Lester put his hands into his back pockets, and started to push himself forward. Before I knew it, he had pushed himself up and out of the mud!

While Lester washed off, I explained my latest concern to him.

"We have to get something for Dad, so he won't get so old!" I said. "I heard Mom say that Dad's going to be forty-five years old, and that sounds *awful* old."

"He *is* awful old," agreed Lester. "Why, he has been around here as far back as I can remember."

"What does Dad like better than anything else? Think of something that would make him feel younger," I said.

Lester said, "How come I have to do the thinking?"

I replied, "Don't think for me, think for Dad!"

After thinking, Lester said, "Why not get somebody to shave Dad? Oscar doesn't have whiskers all over his face, and he doesn't look anywhere near as old as Dad does."

This gave me an idea. "Oscar smokes a lot of cigars," I said, "so let's buy Dad some cigars."

"I don't think Dad would give us any money," Lester replied, "but we could get an empty cigar box from Oscar and make some cigars in one of the tobacco barns."

"That's a good idea," I said. "I watched Oscar make some cigars once. He filled a cigar box full, and then put a board on the cigars that just fit into the box. Then he put a fifty-pound weight on the board to press them down for a few days."

Lester jumped in again. "Ya, I have seen Oscar do that, and then he filled up the box again and put the weight back on again and again, until the cigar box was really solid with nice square cigars."

"We've seen Bert *try* to make cigars, and we should ask him how he does it so we don't do the same," I said, laughing.

I hunted up Oscar and asked him, "Why is it that you don't make all of the tobacco in the tobacco barn into cigars?"

"Because I don't want to be a millionaire," was Oscar's mild-mannered reply.

I went back to Lester and asked him, "What is a millionaire?"

"Harold, I just don't want to think that hard for awhile," he said, but then added, "but I will tell you that it sounds like an awful lot of air to me."

Lester and me got real busy and made up a box of cigars the same way we had seen Oscar do it. It took a long while and we were a little late for Dad's birthday, but we finally gave Dad the cigars.

To our surprise, Dad really got mad at us.

"Where did you kids get the money to buy these cigars?" he asked gruffly.

We just stood there, astonished. Mom felt sorry for Lester and me and said, "John, just enjoy your cigars and thank your two little angels for their thoughtfulness. Oscar probably bought the cigars for them, so they could all make you happy and you in turn could make them happy."

Me and Lester were awful proud of the cigars we had made, because Dad had mistaken them for store-bought. We talked about this and decided to make it a point not to talk to Bert for a few days, because whenever Bert made a cigar, we always had to ask him, "What is it?" We knew that once we got started we couldn't resist taunting him, and he would get mad and chase us. Then Gussy would run alongside of all of us and get awful tired, and then go back and bark at Bert. I know this sounds odd, but we felt it was best not to rub Bert's nose in it, for ol' Gussy's sake.

|18|

BERT AND THE EAGLE

Brother Bert always seemed to be spying on us. He would tell Mom and Dad about everything we did, and about some things we didn't do.

When Bert was ten he had three or four small steel traps that he used to capture 'coons and skunks. He set them just above the large pasture in the beautiful woods that we could see from the house.

One day Bert went out to check his traps. Soon we saw him running down from the lower edge of the woods with something really big stuck to the top of his head. He was also carrying something in his hands.

When he got closer we could see that Bert was carrying a fence post in his hands, and he had a large bird clinging to his head!

"That is a Golden Eagle!" said Oscar, before Dad could get the same words out.

"It looks like some of the eagle's claws are caught in a steel trap that Bert fastened to the fence post with a chain," Dad said.

We all ran out to meet Bert in the backyard.

"Poor Bert has met his match," Dad muttered. "It serves him right for setting out those damn steel traps."

Dad ran to the tool shop and put on his heavy blacksmith's gloves. To Oscar he shouted, "Go to the livestock barn and get a nose bag!"—a heavy canvas bag that can be attached to a horse's head that a horse eats grain from. To Lester Dad said, "Run to the kitchen and bring back a kitchen chair for Bert to sit on." Lester raced up with the chair, and Dad grabbed it and told Bert to sit down.

Every few seconds the big Golden Eagle would try to fly away with the trap and the chain, but with his claws still stuck in Bert's scalp. Then the eagle would sit back down on Bert's head.

There was lots of blood on Bert's head, face, and on his front and back sides. He winced with pain while the eagle's big wings beat on Dad and Oscar.

Finally Dad was able to grab the head of the Golden Eagle and cover it with the nose bag. He told Oscar to hang onto both the bag and the eagle's body.

Dad then unhooked, very painfully for Bert, the eagle's talons, one at a time. The eagle had only one talon caught in Bert's trap.

Bert and the Golden Eagle were both confined for a few days until their wounds healed. Bert got the worst of it, and he took much longer to heal.

Bert, once he got his wits together, told us about the part we didn't see. "The Golden Eagle," he said, "started to fly at the first sight of me. It lifted the thirty-pound locust fence post up into the air about ten feet, along with the chain and the trap, and then couldn't get any higher. I ran as fast as I could and managed to get under the eagle. The eagle was tiring and gradually got lower and lower until I was able to jump up and grab the end of the post to pull it down."

Bert winced at the next part: "Then the eagle landed on my head. He stuck his free talons deep into my scalp. Every few seconds he would try to fly away, only to return to bury his talons in my scalp."

Bert, being very young, did not realize the power and viciousness of this large wild bird, and found himself at the mercy of the eagle.

When the time came to release the Golden Eagle to his freedom, the whole family and all the hired help gathered together back up in the woods. We cheered the beautiful sight of this magnificent Golden Eagle taking flight into the sunny Indiana sky. Even Bert, still hurting from his injuries, had the pleasure of seeing it. It was a wondrous sight to us.

|19|

THE FISH THAT SAVED MY LIFE

Night fishing was one of the most thrilling things I could think of, but often I got left behind because I was too young. But there were plenty of other things to do that I enjoyed.

In the evening after supper, our family found pleasure in listening to Dad read the daily newspapers. We took the *Chicago Tribune*, *The Indianapolis Times Star*, *The Cincinnati Post*, and *The Brookville Democrat*.

He would read all of the comics from the four major newspapers to Lester and me. That was a lot of reading, especially in the Sunday papers. He did a lot of laughing while reading the comics, and so did we.

Under Mom's supervision, I would often have my legs poked into the cookstove's oven with the door pulled open. My legs rested on two wooden boards, soaking up the heat. I had been born with rheumatoid arthritis, the kind that hangs around all of one's life. The heat sure felt good on my joints.

Dad read all of the articles of interest to us, including the war news, even if we didn't want to listen. He knew that some of it would be retained by us kids.

Among other things we did in the evenings, we played the Cecilian Record Player or listened to the old hand organ upstairs. Sometimes a neighbor would come over and play a few good tunes on his harmonica. Dad was a good fiddler and a good singer, often singing in different trios and quartets.

One evening when I was six years old, after Dad had read the comics and current events to us, Bert said, "Dad, will you let Harold go fishing with me tonight at the pond?"

Dad was reluctant but finally agreed to let me go. The pond was a half-mile from the house, and was always good for bass and catfish.

It was a beautiful moonlit night, so we didn't need a lantern. Bert and me took off all of our clothes before we got into the pond. This way, our clothes would be nice and dry for the trip home.

We took a fourteen-foot-long net to pull back and forth across the mud bottom that was about three hundred feet across. We raised it occasionally to take out a fish or two.

We were having good luck, but our bare feet were getting sore and aching from stepping on catfish. They would become frightened and bury themselves in the mud. The horns on their gills are poisonous.

"I feel the net jerking again," said Bert. "Let's raise it up."

We did and it looked like we had five or six big fish. In the moonlight we saw something else in the net that didn't look so nice.

"*Water moccasin!*" yelled Bert.

The big snake was almost against his bare belly. He quickly raised his end of the net above his face. All of those slick fish and that damn water moccasin slid to my end of the net.

That monstrous, poisonous snake was now against *my* belly and trying to climb up on top of me. I have always liked snakes, but this one suited me too well. I can still see that water moccasin's mean-looking eyes and head while it was striking at the flopping fish.

In fact, it was the fish that saved my life.

I was very lucky the snake didn't strike at me when I dropped my end of the net and scrambled away. Bert still had his end of the net held high above his tall body. He was also uttering some fancy swear words at me.

"We just lost the best catch of the night because of that damn snake and you!" he said in disgust.

For a long time after that fishing nightmare, every time Bert got the fishing net and tried to get up a night-fishing party, I would disappear into one of my best hiding places.

|20|

THE NIGHT OF THE GHOSTS

One day Mom said, "Some of our relatives are coming to visit with us, Harold, so you will have to sleep with Bert upstairs."

I knew that meant trouble, and asked Mom, "Why with *Bert?*"

"Never mind," Mom replied. "I need your beds."

The first night with Bert was a doozer—he pulled the covers in his sleep. Our temporary bed was a folding-bed couch with no headboard or footboard. It had a two-foot-wide hinged extension on each side that could be let down.

I pulled the covers back. He pulled them his way. This went on for awhile, and neither of us got any sleep.

Bert said, "We'll have to do something about this cover-pulling."

"You woke me up by pulling *my* covers," I said.

"I did not," argued Bert. "You wasn't asleep, as your eyes were open."

"How can you tell in the dark?" I asked.

Bert laughed wildly, and then growled. "I am a tiger, and can see in the dark!"

There was a long silence.

Then Bert kicked me square in my back with his knee. "You've got to quit pulling covers!" he snarled.

Lying on the very edge of this unfamiliar bed, bruised and shivering from the cold, I finally suggested a compromise.

"Why don't we sleep closer together?" I asked. "Then we won't be pulling covers."

Bert, being unpredictable, leaped over on top of me. His weight was too much for the flimsy bed, and we both landed on the floor with the bed on top of us.

I scrambled out from under it and jumped to my feet. I was completely turned around and frightened. I headed for the door, but ran over a low table with lots of Mom's things on it.

Meanwhile, Bert stood up only to fall over the upside-down bed. He got up again and fell over the same table I had tripped on. The noise was terrible. The houses in those days were built like sounding boards in pianos.

The entire household was now awake or half-awake. Dad thought it was something outside, since Gussy was barking. Dad grabbed his double-barreled shotgun and ran outside in his snow-white long johns. He ran smack into Mom's new clothesline, with some of her sheets hanging on it.

Dad fell over backwards, and the ten-gauge cannon fired one barrel. Mom, still only half-awake, found her way outside to see what Dad was shooting at. All she could see was something unnatural running toward the back gate.

In his long johns, Dad looked like a headless and footless ghost, waving something white in the air. By now, Mom was scared and hysterical. She screamed and ran back into the house.

Our visiting relatives apparently thought it wise to stay huddled together in their rooms.

About that time, Oscar arrived in the dark kitchen in his white long johns. In the darkness he looked like another ghost to Mom. Screaming again, she ran back outside. Oscar ran after her, trying to tell her it was just him.

Dad, still outside and confused, dimly saw what looked like a ghost chasing after Mom. This made Dad angry and frightened. He fired the other barrel of his shotgun into the air. By pure accident, he hit the big dinner bell that was hung twenty feet above on a long post.

The noise from the ten-gauge and then from the dinner bell was just too much for Mom to take. She fainted.

Dad ran into the house for more shotgun shells and a lantern. When he returned he saw Mom on the ground and lit the lantern so he could find out about Mom's condition.

Oscar, still out in the darkness, didn't want to get shot by accident, so he ran to the livestock barn and hid out until daylight. When the sun came up, he quietly made his way back to his room and his clothes without further incident.

The big noise and mess was never solved either by the

folks or by our astonished relatives. Bert and me quickly cleaned up our bedroom and remade our bed. When the folks looked into our room, they thought we were sound asleep.

We never told anybody we had started all of the ghostly commotion in the first place. We didn't have any more trouble sleeping together upstairs, but we were very grateful when the relatives left. Just getting back into our own beds was wonderful.

For years, Bert and me couldn't stand to stay and listen when the folks started to tell about the mysterious night when the ghost chased Mom and she fainted, and when Dad fired his ten-gauge shotgun at the dinner bell with a sheet wrapped around the end of the barrels. Me and Bert would just quietly get up and leave the house so our grins and laughing wouldn't give away our secret.

|21|

FOX VS. CROWS

Almost every day, Bert, Lester, and me roamed far and wide along the creeks, river, or woods. We saw many wonders of nature in all kinds of weather. We found lots of snakes, turtles, and other animals of all kinds.

Bert, after he saw the big zoo in Indianapolis, wanted to put everything in cages, but that was against Dad's will.

Bert found a large crow's nest and came home with two naked crow babies. I thought they were the ugliest things I had ever seen.

But Dollie said, "Oh, they are so beautiful! I am going to name them 'Maggie' and 'Jiggs'"—the names of two popular characters in the comics. And, of course, she got to keep them.

Dollie put them in a box behind the cookstove to keep them warm. Mom and Dad didn't say much since nobody in Indiana liked crows except my sister. Dollie looked after Maggie and Jiggs in great style.

One day, Bert came home from digging in a fox hole. He brought with him one tiny red fox pup.

Dad saw it and asked, "Were there any more pups?"

"I could hear more pups yipping back in the den," Bert answered.

After giving Bert everything but a thrashing, Dad said, "You may keep this one, but don't go back to the den. Mother Fox will have moved the pups to a new location." He added, "You must stay forever away from them."

Bert was very happy with his new young pet, and soon named him Digger. Digger grew up to be a beautiful red fox. Bert released Digger in our fenced-in yard with a long, light rope attached to his collar.

We soon found out that Digger liked chickens. We kept the chicken-house door closed during the night, when Digger was allowed to run loose. Even if a fox isn't hungry, it will still kill chickens. So Digger was always tied up in our backyard during the day.

Dollie always kept Maggie and Jiggs behind the cookstove at night. A disaster was in the making. Somehow, the kitchen door was not always completely closed and locked at night. One fatal night it came open and Digger was not about to miss a chance to get at Maggie and Jiggs.

When Mom came downstairs to start breakfast, the only things left of Maggie and Jiggs were a few little black feathers on the kitchen floor.

This became a disaster for all time when Dollie came down to feed her beloved pets and found them gone. She immediately charged Bert with murder, and vowed to get revenge on Digger.

The feud got so bitter, and Dollie got so violent, that my brother and sister started to fight, and Dad had to separate them.

After thinking for awhile, Dad said, "Bert, you really *do* owe Dollie something." At the same time, Dad felt sorry for Bert.

Dollie had a suggestion: "Maybe you should have a fur piece made for me *from Digger's hide.*"

Bert's temper flashed. "Never. Never. I could *never* stand seeing Digger's fur around your neck."

After a week or so, Dollie's fury had calmed. But another storm was just over the horizon. Oscar came to Dad with a half-eaten one-week-old pig from highly prized purebred stock.

"The little pig had been carried from its pen," said Oscar, "and there were fox tracks all around it."

Inspection of the fur around Digger's mouth revealed traces of blood.

Dollie was standing nearby and overheard the discussion. She immediately cornered Bert.

"Now you *have* to kill that fox," she said, "because he is now killing little pigs, just like he killed my beautiful Maggie and Jiggs."

Dad and Oscar gathered the evidence and went to Bert. Dad told Bert, "In a few weeks, when the weather gets colder and the fur is prime, you must have a fur piece made from Digger's hide for your sister." Oscar added, "If you were a grown man, you would certainly have to pay for a very valuable dead pig."

Bert was deeply hurt. A few nights later he took Digger, without anyone knowing about it, three miles into what was called Banes Woods, and freed his pet fox.

He hoped that Digger would like it in the woods and would not return home. Bert turned his lantern down low and made his way back home. On the back door step, he found poor ol' Digger happily waiting for him.

For weeks, Bert tried desperately to get Digger to leave home, while at the same time he tried hard to find some other way to compensate Dollie and Oscar.

All of his efforts were in vain. Digger could not be saved. He is long gone now, but the fur neck piece made from his hide is still beautiful today, and still brings back many bittersweet memories.

|22|

WILD DOINGS IN THE DARK

"Let's go 'coon hunting tonight," Bert said to me. For some reason I got very excited. I fed Gussy so she could stand the hunt. Bert cleaned a lantern and filled the bowl with kerosene.

The night was moonless. When we reached Mr. Mulford's hillside pasture about a mile from home, Gussy treed something far off in a clump of trees. Bert said nothing, turned the lantern light down low, and took off running toward Gussy's barking. I couldn't keep up with him, and quickly found myself left behind in total darkness.

Gussy quit barking after awhile. I was tired, and had to walk very slowly on the strange hillside pasture. Then I heard a low thundering sound. It was coming down the hill and getting closer and closer to me.

I could dimly see a huge white mass divide above me on the hill, then thunder around me on each side. The frightening sound passed me by, and soon it disappeared below me on the hill.

I was so scared I couldn't move. Then, far away, Bert turned up his lantern light and I spotted it. I ran in that direction, crying and falling down in the dark, until I got to him.

Angry and bleeding, I said to him, "Damn you, Bert, why did you leave me alone in the dark?"

Bert shrugged, "When ol' Gussy barks, you gotta run fast to her or she will give up and leave what she's got treed."

While he talked, he was too busy to look at me. He was poking a long stick into a hollow, half-rotten log.

I started to tell Bert about that white mass that frightened me, and how it divided and went around me on each side making a terrible thundering noise. Bert thought that was the funniest thing he had ever heard. He laughed and poked and poked and laughed.

"That was a herd of sheep, dummy. I saw them in my lantern light when I was running," he said. "I must've scared them on my way over to find Gussy."

Bert pulled his long stick out of the hollow log, got out his pocketknife, and split the end of the stick two ways. He opened up the splits slightly and wedged them open with tiny sticks.

My indignation died down as my curiosity grew. Finally I asked, "Whatcha doing that for?"

With a smart attitude, Bert answered, "This will show me, dummy, what's inside that hollow log. I know it ain't no skunk," he laughed, "because we would know by now if it was by the stink!"

Bert carefully poked his stick back into the log. He said, "It's against something." He twisted the stick around several times, pulled it out and looked at the hairs that were caught in the split end.

"It's a possum!" he announced.

Bert handed me a gunnysack, and told me to hold it over the end of the log. He started probing in the other end of the log, and Gussy ran up and started to bark again. I started getting a lot of something wiggly in my gunnysack.

"Bert," I yelled, "I think that's all of whatever it is!"

We looked into the gunny sack, but couldn't be sure what all we had in there because of the dim lantern light. The next morning we opened the sack and dumped a total of twenty-four possums out.

Dad looked into Mommy Possum's pouch.

"She has two litters," he said. "One litter is still hanging onto the nipples, while the other litter—they're each about five inches long—is running loose and following her."

Bert put them in a big dark wooden cage and fed them for four days. We never saw them eat, but they did.

Finally Dad said, "You two take all of the possums back to that hollow log. Put them in it tonight when it's cool."

We were very reluctant, but we knew it was the right thing to do, so we did it.

|23|

CLOWNS AND CRAWDADS

Dad didn't realize that our backyard animal world was destined to drive him nuts. Me and Lester already had a cage filled with fourteen snakes and two turtles hidden under a rosebush.

Some of the snakes were poisonous, but we knew which ones they were. We had water moccasins, copperheads, and spreading vipers, which are distant cousins of the cobra.

To add to Dad's misery, Walter Cummins gave us two young raccoons.

"My dogs killed their mother," he explained. "These two are just too young to survive on their own."

Dad took the young 'coons, but Mr. Cummins darn-near lost his job over it. Dad openly reminded him to never again hunt 'coons or anything else on his farm with professional hunting dogs.

We named the two 'coons Mutt and Jeff after two famous newspaper comic characters. Mom fed them a mixture of honey and milk and kept them in the house for three months. They never saw the inside of a cage and made wonderful entertaining clowns for all of us.

I liked going with Mutt and Jeff down to Pipe Creek to swim together in the Old Whirl Hole. The Whirl Hole was about twenty-two feet deep and about one hundred feet across in any direction. It was usually calm and safe to swim in, but sometimes a big rainstorm would turn it into a raging, twisting torrent of muddy water.

After a swim with me, Mutt and Jeff would search for food in the shallows by feeling everything on the bottom of the creek until they found crawdads, which look like little lobsters.

The 'coons would roll a little crawdad around on the bottom until he would surrender to them. Then he would become part of their dinner.

When Mutt and Jeff were rolling a crawdad with their front feet, they would look me right in the face or look up at the sky or at anything else with no expression at all on their faces. They never looked down at that poor ol' crawdad, to see what they were doing to it. I guess they were chicken-hearted and couldn't stand to see their own cruelty.

Everything they ate they washed first by rubbing it in the water with both front feet. The 'coons were very clean little animals.

When the season for wild blackberry picking arrived, we prepared big picnic dinners, which always included pies and coffee. We would set out walking to the largest berry patches with everyone carrying something. The whole family had to pick berries.

Of course Gussy came, too, along with Just Plain Cat and our 'coons, Mutt and Jeff. Nearly everything except the live-stock went. Dad always said, "We must look like Coxey's rag-tag army strung out along the hillside trail." Mom always said, "Now don't pick the red berries—a blackberry is red when it is green!"

One day when we had all been busy picking berries for several hours, we heard Lester say, "Look! Right here I can pick more blackberries off the ground than off the bushes."

"How did so many berries get on the ground?" asked Oscar. Someone in the family, who was not talking, had hung our extra big bucket full of berries on a high limb of a tree, thinking the 'coons wouldn't find it there.

Everyone looked up and there was ol' Mutt sitting in the big bucket slinging berries everywhere. Jeff was rocking the bucket, trying to dump Mutt out. Before anyone could save the rest of the bucket of precious berries that represented hours of work, down it came tumbling to the grass.

This was, to my recollection, one of the few times I saw these two 'coons at the brink of destruction. Poor Dad couldn't say anything we could understand—he couldn't think of words bad enough to use.

At night, Mutt and Jeff would bring crawdads in from Pipe Creek. They would scratch and cry at the back door until some-one would get up to let them in. Their crawdads were confis-cated at the door and put alive into a can for feeding later on.

This routine was getting to Dad. One day Dad said to Lester and me, "Why don't you boys catch crawdads during the day to feed to the 'coons?"

We did this, but the 'coons didn't catch on. They just kept scratching and crying at the back door with their own crawdad catches. And Dad still had to be a slave to Mutt and Jeff.

"No more of this!" Dad said one day, ordering everyone to ignore them at night.

Everything went well until one night when those little rascals discovered the downspout. It carried rainwater from the roof just under Dad and Mom's upstairs window. The pipe joined up with another at the corner, then ran on down to the ground.

The night was warm and rainy. Mom and Dad slept under only one sheet with their window open. Jeff had caught a big crawdad with huge pincers. He carried it with him as he quietly crawled up the downspout and into the bedroom. He was soaking wet. Clutching his crawdad, he tried to crawl under the sheet between Mom and Dad.

Dad woke up, and with a lot of swearing that woke us all up too, he grabbed ol' Jeff. Without pity he slung the wet 'coon out of the open window. Jeff plunked down on the ground below and Mutt came over to him to see if he could help put some air back into his lungs.

Half-asleep and happy that this tussle was over, Mom and Dad returned to bed. The rest of us calmed down and drifted off to sleep again, too.

Suddenly a loud squall startled all of us back to our senses. Jeff had left his big crawdad under the sheet, and it had a hold of Dad someplace!

Mom, awake again, helped take the monster off of Dad, but she never told us where it was attached. However, Dad's face would change colors whenever Mom would teasingly hint about the story to her friends and neighbors.

Mutt and Jeff lived with us for over five years, until one night a neighbor went out hunting with two 'coon dogs and treed Mutt and shot him.

Later, he told Mom, "When I looked at the dead 'coon, I

knew instantly it was Mutt." He felt real bad and offered Mom forty dollars, which was a lot of money in those days. Mom turned it down.

"It would be like taking money for a dead member of the family," she said.

Mom did take Mutt's body, so he would have a proper grave up on the hill. Jeff stayed around for a short time and left, only to return and leave again for short periods. This went on for nearly a year, until one time when ol' Jeff never returned.

Our whole family missed these beautiful little clowns that had made our lives so rich and full of laughter.

|24|

FROM GUSSY TO LUMMOX

Gussy, our faithful dog, was old and pregnant, a bad combination, but she had her puppies with apparently no ill effects. When old enough, all of the puppies were given away, except the largest one. He was brown and was very awkward, oversized and lazy. Mom named him Lummox.

Lummox never did lie down. He would simply relax while standing and fall down.

One day I saw him chasing a rabbit. It would stop often to let him catch up. Lummox lost track of that rabbit whenever it made a sharp turn. He just kept going straight until he stalled out. Of course, he never caught that rabbit or any other one.

Lummox was the only dog I ever saw that let his tail hang down while wagging it. If he could, he would lean up against something while standing. Lummox never complained about anything, probably because it was just too tiring.

One day poor Gussy was seen snapping at the chickens. She was acting strange to us kids and we had never seen this before. Dad saw her later in the yard going in circles and foaming at the mouth. Gussy had gotten the dreaded disease hydrophobia. Dad called Oscar and told him.

"I don't think I can carry out the job of relieving her of her misery," said Dad sorrowfully.

Dad saw me trying to play with Gussy and quickly took me into the house.

"Best leave ol' Gussy alone," he said. "She is very sick."

Oscar said, "It's going to be a hard job for me to do, Dad. But if you need a favor this big, you shall have it."

Feeling very bad, Oscar picked up a hickory bull stick and attached its harness snap on Gussy's collar so he could keep Gussy at arm's length and not be bitten by her. Oscar told Dad, "Keep the kids in the house, and give me a gun." Dad handed him the twenty-two rifle.

They buried Gussy on a hilltop meadow across Pipe Creek. Dad and Oscar placed a white limestone marker over her grave.

After Lester and I found out what had happened to her, we visited her grave often. We would stay awhile and talk about good ol' Gussy.

We were glad that Gussy had given us Lummox. He looked a lot like her, but he was never the playmate that she was. I guess he was just too lazy.

|25|

SCHOOL LEARNING

When I first heard about crystal balls, I tried to get Mom to buy me a powerful one. I wanted to see what was in the future. With a crystal ball I thought I could separate the good from the bad. And best of all, I wouldn't have to go to school. I would get rich and tell all of my friends how they could do it, too.

Mom smiled and said, "You have to get very rich to afford a crystal ball like that, and then you would not need one."

I told Lester about it, and he said, "I know where there's an old cannon ball, and *they* are awful powerful."

Mom couldn't get school out of her head, and I couldn't get it into my head. Lester said, "You better go to school, 'cause if you don't go to school, Mom will get awful mean, maybe mean enough to whip you, and when she whips you, she always whips me!"

I was six and in grade one. I didn't like school much. It took up too much of my very important time, and I just couldn't figure out how it could help me when I was already doing so well. "My brothers and sister are accidentally teaching me everything I need to know, including spelling, reading, writing, arithmetic, and geography," I told Mom. "Why, I learn just by listening to them talk!" She said I needed school to help me improve my spelling and grammar. I argued that my grammar would improve naturally as time went by.

But Mom won. I had to walk to Elm Grove, a little one-room country school one mile away, with my brothers and sister. When the road was dry or snow-covered, I could walk, run, jump, or creep to school by myself. When it was wet, however, I couldn't get through the deep mud in the road, so Bert and Dollie would put me between them and drag me, sometimes almost the whole mile, until we reached the school.

This country school had grades from first through tenth, all taught by one lady teacher.

School "learned" me one thing fast, and that was how to fight. At first I didn't know what a kid wanted when he would hit me in the back. When I caught on to what the rascals wanted, I would fight like a tiger. And that is what they started calling me, "Ol' Tiger." I liked fighting so well that all the rascals who were left quit the sport.

One big student, by the name of Stanley C., was a nice young man. He was the only student in the tenth grade with black whiskers. He said he had never shaved in his life.

Stanley was our close neighbor. One day he told me, "I am old enough to be your daddy." Sometimes Ol' Stanley would put me on top of his head and run all over the school grounds, making scary noises and acting like a crazed and disoriented wild bull.

I loved it—it was my favorite thing at school.

|26|

OUR TEACHER DEFIES GRAVITY

I found that teasing the young lady teacher was fun. One day, when no one was in the classroom except me, I spotted the teacher's low-cut overshoes. I threw one against the white plastered wall, just for fun. It left a perfect footprint.

I looked carefully at the sole of her overshoe and found it had a lot of floor oil and dust mixed on it. Every time it hit the wall just right, it would leave a track, but would leave nothing if it hit any other way. I kept trying until I got a footprint.

I guess my inventiveness was showing. As best I could, I wiped out the tracks that I had already made on the wall. Then I started with both overshoes, making the left and right tracks of our teacher walking up the wall, across the ceiling, and down the other side. When the tracks showed up a little dim, I rubbed the soles of her overshoes on the oily floor. Of course, not all of the tracks were in their proper places, but this made it even funnier. I was afraid I would be seen, so as soon as I could I ran outside. I thought I would never be able to control my laughter.

The bell rang, and all the kids went into the classroom. Most of them started laughing, but some of them, the smart ones, were puzzled because they were sure the teacher's overshoes had made the tracks since they were larger than the footwear that we wore.

They stared at the walls and ceiling. Everyone studied hard and wondered how our lady teacher could have done that trick of walking up the wall, across the ceiling, and down the other wall. Even our teacher gave up after awhile and started laughing with us.

This trick that I pulled on that sweet little teacher was almost regrettable because she was never able to explain it to us kids or to the parents. We all loved her.

I never did tell her or anyone else that I did it. If my Dad had found it out, he would have personally "keelhauled" me behind the Maxwell for hours on end, and then stood me up to see if I made a shadow. To my knowledge, no one has ever solved this mystery.

One day the country schoolhouse at Elm Grove was destroyed by fire. While visiting in Indiana recently, I noticed that the old school pump was still standing. It looked like it might still be usable, with a little work.

|27|

NEAR DISASTER ABOVE PIPE CREEK

After the little one-room school at Elm Grove burned down, we were all hauled by horse-drawn school wagon to the Metamora town school, eight miles from our house. We lived at the very end of the school wagon route.

It was dark in the mornings when we left for the town school and it was dark in the evenings when we arrived home. The school wagon had two kerosene lanterns hung on the front outside corners to provide light.

One morning an old man by the name of Mr. Morgan was driving a team of mules on our school wagon. Not far from our house the road was packed solid with ice. The road sloped toward Pipe Creek, raging about eighty or one hundred feet below. I was the only kid on the wagon.

Worried, Mr. Morgan stopped his mules and got out in the dark. He removed a lantern from the front corner of the wagon and used it to look over the icy spot.

Inside the school wagon there were no lights, only a kerosene heater. I went to the front end of the wagon and looked out. I could see the dangerous ice-covered road lit up by Mr. Morgan's lantern. I was now scared and retreated to the back of the wagon.

Mr. Morgan reattached the lantern, got back in the driver's seat, and hollered to his trusty mules to start pulling for dear life. The mules wore rough-shod shoes for ice, and they were pulling real good.

Suddenly the back end of the wagon began to slide off the road. In the darkness all I saw was the hot kerosene heater sliding directly toward me.

I thought the school wagon might catch on fire. I jumped up on the seats to keep from being burned. Somehow I grabbed a leather strap hanging down from the roof and took a death grip on it.

My next thought was that the whole thing, mules and all, was going to tumble a hundred feet down into Pipe Creek, but those trusty ol' mules brayed and buried their inch-long steel corks into the ice. They must have pulled with every ounce of strength they could muster. They literally lifted the heavy school wagon almost straight up and back onto the ice-covered road. To my relief, the fire stayed inside the kerosene heater.

A short distance farther, where there was no ice, the mules got a well-deserved rest. Mr. Morgan filled their nose bags with grain to thank them and to give them added strength to pull our heavy school wagon the rest of the way.

Mr. Morgan then came back to me. He gave me some words of comfort and a love pat on the back to try to make me feel that everything was fine with the world.

I will never forget the terrible experience of being all alone in the dark wagon on that early morning ride to the Metamora town school.

|28|

THE LAW AGAINST MURDER

One day I almost caused a disaster myself when I was alone in the house with Dollie. She was busy in the kitchen and had a fire going in the cookstove.

I found some of Dad's ten-gauge shotgun shells. I took

them to the tool shop and removed the shot and gunpowder from them.

After carefully examining the shotgun, I decided I could make my own gun by loading the gun powder in a one-foot-long heavy gas pipe. I threaded a cap on one end, packed the powder, wadding, and shot in the other end, and tamped it in solid.

The big gun was now ready to fire. My only problem was how to do it. Very heavy thinking was necessary, so I went back into the kitchen to think.

I saw Dollie putting wood into the cookstove. That alerted my inventive mind, and what I did next almost caused a real disaster. What I had made was actually a dangerous pipe bomb, something I had never heard of before.

I waited for Dollie to leave the house. I could sense trouble, maybe real trouble, but my desire for the excitement of this experiment overwhelmed me. I threw all caution to the wind. I waited for a long time, then when Dollie headed for the outhouse, my chance arrived.

I hurried to the big kitchen stove and removed one of the round lids. I could see the glowing hot coals, and I placed the pipe gun under them, pointing it at the open kitchen door. I replaced the stove lid just as Dollie suddenly entered the kitchen.

I was scared and couldn't say anything. I hadn't planned on her being back so soon.

Dollie took one of the stove lids off to add three pieces of stove wood to the fire. She replaced the lid without noticing my pipe gun. She was standing three feet to the right side of the cookstove, and that may have saved her life. I ran to push her away just as a terrifying explosion blew away the left side of the stove and firebox.

One of the stove lids went up through the double ceiling into the upstairs bedroom. The stove grates were blown down into what was left of the ash pan. Small fires started to burn all over the kitchen because the burning wood flew in all directions.

The explosion was heard by everyone on the Hannebaum farm. Dad, Mom, my brothers, and all the hired help came running into the smoky shambles. They extinguished the small fires that were burning in the kitchen. One particularly troublesome piece of burning wood was stuck inside the double ceiling. The blackened mess left was unbelievable.

Dollie was in shock with minor cuts and bruises. I survived the explosion far better than I did Mom and Dad's onslaught. The only thing that kept them from killing me was the law against murder.

It was years before Dollie would forgive me for my experiment that day.

|29|

GEORGE SHEBLER, INVENTOR

Dad and Mom were very good friends with a man from Indianapolis, a millionaire bachelor by the name of George Shebler, the inventor of the famous Shebler Float-Type Carburetor.

Mr. Shebler got the idea for his invention when he saw an automatic watering trough for hogs. When the hogs drank water out of this trough, a hollow float made from galvanized iron would drop down to the new lower water level and allow water in. When the rising float reached the high water level, it would shut off the water. This float was located at one end of the trough, and the mechanism was protected by a cage so the hogs couldn't damage it.

His carburetor was introduced to the automobile industry by Wilhelm Maybach, a German engineer and inventor of the honeycomb radiator, in 1892. Both Shebler's carburetor and Maybach's radiator are still used throughout the world.

Shebler's invention was the first float and jet atomized-fuel system. Without this ingenious device, the internal combustion gasoline engine could not have survived the competition created by diesel engines and others.

Among his cars, Mr. Shebler owned a yellow Mercer, a Duesenberg built in nearby Connersville, Indiana, a Stutz Bear

Cat, and a Cadillac. He also owned and piloted his own biplane. Us kids saw the biplane only once, when it flew low
over the north end of Dad's farm and gave us and all of the
livestock a big scare.

Mr. Shebler and Dad did a lot of fishing together. They
went to many different places in the hill country of Indiana to
fish and hunt. They were real buddies.

When Mr. Shebler was at our place, Mom would always
cook up a tasty dinner for him. Dad would occasionally hand
him a box of his specially made cigars. As for Lester and me,
we would load up Mr. Shebler's yellow Mercer with large watermelons from Dad's melon patch. In return, Mr. Shebler
would give Lester and me some candy or money. I later learned
that he and Dad would unload about half of the melons when
we were not looking, and Mr. Shebler would be off for the big
city of Indianapolis.

Mr. Shebler always gave Dollie something special when
he visited us. Believe it or not, these gifts included a fine fur
piece, a diamond necklace, and a diamond brooch—and Dollie was only sixteen at the time. Mom was always speechless
and at first couldn't believe that these gifts were real.

Although Mr. Shebler never told us, Dad and Mom found
out by reading the newspapers that he owned a controlling
interest in the Indianapolis Speedway, as it was called at that
time. Today this automobile racing track is the location of the
Indianapolis 500 or Indy 500. Mr. Shebler also owned large
interests in manufacturing.

As the story was told to me, when Mr. Shebler was a kid
his family was very poor and they could afford very little. One
day when he was about eleven years old, George went into a
little country store wearing no shoes or shirt and with only a
ragged pair of overalls on. The store owner knew his parents
and felt sorry for him. He gave George a complete new outfit
to wear, including shoes, and offered him a job in his store.
George was so happy that he ran over a mile home to tell his
parents about his new job and clothes. Then he ran all the way
back to the store and told the owner, "I want the job."

Mr. Shebler worked at the store for several years and saved

all of his money, which he used to invent and patent his float-style carburetor.

About twenty years later, George Shebler went back to see if that little store was still there. It was, and it was still being run by the same people, now two decades older.

George was surprised that they still remembered him. They assured him that they loved him as a kid, and their love for him had grown stronger over the years. They were happy for him and proud of his success.

George Shebler not only bought out their store at an over-priced figure, but also set up a lifelong monthly income for them which was far more than they could spend. George had made similar arrangements for his folks, too. He was considered a great man by all who knew him, not just for his inventive mind or for the way he changed the world, but particularly for the kind way he treated his family, friends, and associates.

Over the years, Mom began to notice Mr. Shebler making side-glances at Dollie—more of them each time he visited us. Mom and Dad talked privately about the age difference and decided that Mr. Shebler, like most men, just loved to look at pretty girls.

One morning while visiting at our place, Mr. Shebler asked Mom, "Would you mind if I take Dollie to Indianapolis with me? I will bring her home tonight."

George Shebler was so good to us that Mom couldn't say no, but she didn't say yes either. What she said was, "You'll have to speak to John about it."

Dollie went off with Mr. Shebler to the big city in his yellow Mercer, and they were back that same evening. Mom and Dad were not concerned about her safety—a girl was far safer in those days than she is today. The boy and the girl were equally afraid of each other. The consequences were also much worse then for a man who misbehaved.

Dollie was just too happy to talk for awhile, then said, "George took me up in his airplane." Mr. Shebler sat listening with a big smile.

"I saw beautiful Indianapolis," Dollie said. "It was way down below, with all of its tiny houses and tiny streets. We did a loop-the-loop, too. Mom, you should have been with us. It was the most fun I ever had!"

Dollie's last comment made Mr. Shebler's day. He finally spoke up, saying, "Well, we will do this more often."

Mr. Shebler had supper with us that evening, and both Mom and Dad noticed he and Dollie talking and looking at each other more than usual. Evidently Cupid had shot his arrow into their hearts and love was blossoming.

After that they were with each other many, many times. Dollie continued to receive beautiful gifts. I was particularly impressed with a German silver fishing reel with real rubies for the jewel bearings, and a fine fishing rod with a pearl-inlaid handle.

Once Mr. Shebler drove his yellow Mercer to Daytona Beach, Florida, for a test run of its power and speed. He was there for a few days. On his return he came by our place and reported with a smile, "The Mercer was faster than I thought, but it was a little light for high speed, especially where birds were a hazard."

He added, "I was clocked at 165 miles per hour at times, and the engine had more than enough horsepower. My Duesenberg, however, is more powerful and is probably faster."

When Dollie found out that Mr. Shebler had been to Daytona Beach without asking her to go along, she felt very put out and told Mom, "I don't ever want to see him again."

"Young lady," Mom said, "don't you know you can't go out with a man and stay three or four nights with him? That would be a disgrace to you and to all of us. And if you had a brain in your head, you would know that this is why Mr. Shebler didn't ask you to go with him. Men sometimes like to go off and play with their toys."

Dollie sat pouting and thinking.

"If you love him," Mom went on, "and if he loves you, don't turn him down when he wants to be with you for a day's fun ride or to go to a moving picture show. But you can't go out and stay overnight with him."

She watched Dollie to see if she was hearing what was being said. Dollie sat through a short silence, then finally spoke: "The way you explained it to me, Mom, I now feel a lot better about him going to Daytona Beach without letting me know."

Mom was relieved. "Many troubles invade true love," she told Dollie, "because you care so much. Without love, you don't care nearly as much, and that lets you know when only a friendship exists."

During the summer, Mr. Shebler visited our place many times to fish with Dad, to be with Dollie, and, of course, to put his feet under Mom's supper table.

Whenever he visited with Dollie and our family, he would drive his beautiful yellow Mercer across a deep drain ditch at the end of one of our tobacco-curing barns where he could park it out of the way of our working activities.

One day when me and Lester watched him arrive and bump his nice car over that dangerous, deep ditch again, we sat down on a stack of lumber at the side of the barn to think. I told Lester, "We have to do something about that ditch. I just can't think of what we should do, but you wear a bigger cap than I do, and that means you got more brains than I do."

"Yes, I know that," said Lester, "but be quiet right now because I am trying to figger out what to think about."

After about ten minutes of deep and silent thought, Lester said, "When Dad isn't looking, why don't we drag some of these big boards over to that ditch and build a bridge across it? That way Mr. Shebler can cross the ditch on our bridge and he won't hurt his beautiful car."

"That sounds like a great idea to me," I said happily.

But first, we had an awful job putting Just Plain Cat on top of the barn roof so Lummox would have something to bark at and Dad wouldn't hear us hammering around while we built the bridge.

"How come we have to go to school," I asked Lester admiringly, "when you are already so smart?" Lester replied, "That's easy—it's because of you being so dumb!"

We worked hard and fast on that bridge. Lummox soon turned over his job of barking at Just Plain Cat to two stray dogs and then slept through most of our big construction job.

That evening, we found Mr. Shebler out by the big ditch looking over our bridge. He handed each of us a silver dollar and said, "Thank you gentlemen very sincerely. Your diligent construction endeavors look to be entirely sufficient."

The powerful engine of the beautiful yellow Mercer roared into action. Mr. Shebler headed it toward our untested bridge like a ground-skimming rocket. He must have floored the gas pedal. The beautiful Mercer flashed forward with its wheels spinning out. Splintered planks and boards flew through the air everywhere from the onslaught of the tires, but the magnificent Mercer crossed safely without even a scratch. The whole spectacle made our little black Maxwell look sick.

We saw him wave at Dad and say something. This caused Dad to drop a very big load of stove wood from his arms just so he could wave back.

We knew it would be a lot of interesting work for the two of us to repair and strengthen the bridge in time for Mr. Shebler's next visit, so we went right back to work on it.

|30|

GEORGE AND DOLLIE

Mr. Shebler left for England on a business trip the next day. He also planned to visit relatives in Germany, but by the time he finished his business in England, the war in Europe prevented this.

When he returned home, he came by to see Dollie and to reassure her of his love. He drove his Mercer across our rebuilt bridge, and gave us warm compliments on our engineering job. He told Dad all about his voyage on the Atlantic Ocean. Then he took Dollie into the big city where they made wedding plans and bought an engagement ring. Mom said, "Dollie, your ring has the most beautiful array of diamonds!" My sister would not show it to me and kept it locked in her room when it was not on her finger. I did get one flash from it once as she zipped through the parlor on her way out through the front gate to join Mr. Shebler. Mr. Shebler was having a big laugh with Dad and Oscar. The big laugh was over a box of trick cigars and the fun he'd had in England with some of these special exploding stogies.

A few days later, when more wedding plans were being formulated by the folks, Mom answered a phone call. After a moment she dropped the receiver, lowered her head, and started to cry. She moaned, "Oh no, oh no, oh, my God, no!" Dad grabbed her arm and helped her from the kitchen to the sitting room.

"Flora, what is it that you heard on the telephone?" Dad asked. "What has happened?"

Mom struggled hard to find words and to gather her wits. Finally she said, "The wedding is off." Mom broke down again. Oscar and Dollie were now at her side.

"What is it?" Oscar asked. "Is it bad news?" Oscar then looked through the open door to the kitchen and saw the telephone receiver still hanging down swinging along the wall. He ran to it and tried hard to get an answer, but the telephone was dead at the other end. Mom was still dazed. Dad handed her a pad and pencil. She struggled to control herself, then wrote, "Mr. Shebler is dead, killed by his airplane when it crashed on landing."

Later we received the official news. Mr. George Shebler died while attempting a landing on his private airstrip near Indianapolis during a storm.

The pain from his death lingered for many months for all of us, but especially for Dollie. The shock was devastating to her. Mom was worried about Dollie's condition, and about what long-term effects this tragedy might have on her.

Many of our good neighbors heard about the loss and came to offer sympathy and condolences. Our sadness was gradually dissolved by kind hearts and washed slowly away by gentle laughter.

|31|

OSCAR GOES TO WAR

World War I was raging in Europe between Germany and our Allies in 1917. The government and people of the United States felt obligated to help, but our family could hardly stand the thought that Oscar might be called on to go.

One day it happened. Oscar received a letter drafting him into the service. He took the news better than any of us. He carefully took Dad and Mom out to show them how to take care of his purebred livestock. He taught them how to carry on with all the bookkeeping required for each animal.

Oscar suggested that they hire a young man to help out with the chores. He even suggested that, if he didn't come back, it might be a good idea to sell off the cattle and hogs to help ward off memories and to make the farm easier to run.

Oscar left early one morning from Metamora by train, bound for Camp Sherman in Ohio. We received letters from him daily. This made Mom very anxious to see him. She asked Dad to go with her, but he refused, saying, "It would only make things worse and besides, I am needed to stay home to keep the work going."

Mom and I left by train from Connersville, Indiana. It was my first train ride. I visited every car, talking to nearly everybody aboard about this great train.

The conductor saw my excitement.

"May I show the train to your young son?" he asked Mom.

To my delight, Mom said, "Yes, if you think you are up to it."

At the next stop, the conductor took me outside and gave me some candy to cement our friendship. He showed me the big locomotive that pulled all the cars. He introduced me to the engineer, who took my hand and pulled me up into the cab. The engineer showed me the giant firebox, and held me up to the windows, where I could see the huge, long boiler.

Then he blew the whistle and I couldn't hear anything he said after that.

He motioned to me that I could blow the whistle a short blast, to signal that the train was starting to move away from that station. I did it.

The big engine appeared to be a moving cloud of steam and black smoke as it slowly got under way. The conductor hollered up, as he stepped off to the ground below, and I think he said, "I will tell your Mother where you are!"

I rode to the next town in that giant locomotive with the engineer and the fireman and memorized their every move. I knew that I was the luckiest kid in the whole wide world and would surely grow up to work on a train.

When I got back to Mom, I couldn't talk fast enough, telling her what I had done and what I had seen and how wonderful this train was. I couldn't wait to tell Oscar all about it.

A few hours later we arrived at Camp Sherman. Oscar was happily surprised. He asked me if I had fed ol' Jumbo before we left. Jumbo was a thirteen-hundred-pound pig. I didn't want to talk to Oscar about Jumbo when I could talk to him about that great train ride! Oscar and Mom had a good visit and before I knew it, it was time to go.

We were sad to leave my brother but we promised to visit him again before he left for Europe.

Oscar was later transferred to Camp Taylor, which I think was in Kentucky, for several additional months of training.

It was at Camp Taylor that a soldier went berserk and tried to kill a sergeant who was insulting him and his family, according to Oscar. When he wrote he told us that the soldier's rifle was loaded with five live rounds. The sergeant was running scared and rounding the corner of the barracks when the soldier fired four rounds. One struck the sleeve of the sergeant's coat, one passed through the very corner of the barracks, and two others ripped through the building, shattering and splintering the walls inside.

I visited Oscar again with Mom while he was at Camp Taylor. Oscar showed me the bullet holes that could still be seen in the corner of the barracks.

I was mostly interested in talking about trains, but Oscar

was still interested in talking only about home, family, and livestock.

After we left him, Oscar went on to New York City, where he and several thousand other soldiers boarded the Leviathan, then the world's largest ship. They sailed for Liverpool, England, and later crossed the English Channel to France.

Oscar was assigned to work in the training camps. When he first arrived, he wrote to us and said he could hear explosions and see some of the big long-range shells hit and explode. No one had any idea how long the war might continue.

|32|

ARLIE RUST ARRIVES

Dad and Mom had a big job on their hands now, with Oscar overseas. They decided that help would soon be needed.

One day, Mom saw a redheaded young man outside the front gate petting Lummox. Mom thought she knew him, so she approached and asked, "Aren't you one of the Rust boys?" "Yes," he said. He looked lonely and hungry, so Mom took him into our house. She could tell he had something on his mind.

"Did you want to ask something?" she asked.

He shyly answered, "I have never worked out before, but I need a job, and I sure would like to work for Oscar."

"Oscar went off to the big war," said Mom, almost in tears, "and his return is uncertain."

Mom tried to remember the ages and names of the Rust boys, and soon she guessed, "Are you Arlie Rust?"

"Yes," he said.

Mom said, "You didn't know that Oscar went off to war?"

"No, ma'am," he said. "Why did he go? Oscar couldn't kill anyone."

"He was drafted and had no choice," answered Mom. "Do your folks know you are looking for work?"

"Oh yes," he said. "They know that I am looking for a job."

Mom found Dad and told him Arlie's story. Dad said, "Young man, you are hired to do the chores. I will show you what to do, how to do it, and tell you what your hours will be. We haven't had a chore man since Mr. Koonce died two years ago."

"Arlie, you look hungry," Dad added. "Come with me and we will fix you something to eat."

Arlie was soon a best friend to Lester, Bert, and me. He was the first redhead we had ever seen. Arlie, coming from a large family, sure knew how to get in solid with our whole family and with Mrs. Milbourne. Arlie was a good harmonica player, and he often entertained us.

Arlie's parents and their large family lived just up a steep hill near the schoolhouse. Their house was on Sam Lewis' farm, and Sam didn't charge them any rent. The Rusts didn't have any land and not much money, since they were too religious to make moonshine—which was the only way out of poverty for lots of poor families. Besides, Sam Lewis was religious too, and he would not have let them live in his tenant house if they made moonshine.

Soon after Arlie began to work at our place, Mr. Cummins came over to our house. With a twinkle in his eye, he pointed to Arlie and asked, "Where did you get *that?*"

Mom, her wit encouraged, said, "We didn't—he got us!"

You could tell Arlie wanted to keep his job forever. He learned fast and worked hard. He seemed to be able to do everything on the farm and even helped Mrs. Milbourne in the kitchen. In fact, he would go looking for work to do. In the winter, he learned to work in the curing barns with the tobacco, and he was always good with all the livestock.

|33|

TWO ANGELS VISIT
GRANDPAW AND GRANDMAW

One day Mom took Lester and me out of school and over to Grandpaw and Grandmaw Jones' place. She said, "I don't want you boys to catch the measles that are going around in our school district."

I didn't understand what Mom was talking about, but I didn't mind missing school, so I decided to talk to Lester privately.

"How could we catch the weasels?" I asked him later.

Lester replied, "We are not gonna catch the *weasels*, it's the *measles* that Mom doesn't want us to catch." He added, "I think I could catch one of them things, but you are not near fast enough to catch a measle."

We loved staying with Grandpaw and Grandmaw. They both thought we were little angels and wouldn't correct us. We could do almost anything we wanted to and eat only what we wanted to eat. It was a beautiful life for us at their house.

Grandpaw took us fishing on the second day of our stay. He let us put all our fish worms in the pockets of our overalls. That way we didn't have to carry a bait can, only a fishing pole and a pocketknife. The worms that we didn't use were forgotten about at the end of the day.

We had lots of fish stories to tell Grandmaw that evening and a few fish to show her. It was a fun day.

Our bedroom was cold that night. After an hour or so in bed, Lester got up and said, "I gotta get warm." He put on all of his clothes, even his socks, and went back to bed.

I said, "I'm cold, too, and I am going to do the same." Soon we both warmed up and went off to sleep.

The next morning, Lester and me didn't have to dress. We were already fully clothed and ready for another exciting day with Grandpaw.

But Grandmaw found dead fish worms in our clean bed, and she was extremely angry with Grandpaw. She checked the pockets of our overalls and found more dead worms. She really laid it on Grandpaw for being so senseless about the boys and their fishing worms.

"You must do a lot better today," she told him, "than you did yesterday!"

Lester and me got away scot-free.

After dinner we went exploring out in the barn lot, where there were a few buildings. We found the woodshed, and behind it we found three big oak barrels. They were laid down sideways on a barrel rack. We noticed that each one had a wooden faucet at its lower edge. These wooden barrels were heavy and full of something.

I turned one of the wooden faucets a little, and a small stream of liquid ran out.

"Boy, that smells good," said Lester. He tasted it and added, "Say, it really *is* good!" That did it. We both tried some. We knew that we had never tasted anything like that before!

The barrels rested about one foot off the grassy ground. We tried every way to really drink some. Lester finally got down on his back with his mouth wide open, just where a very small stream would fall right in. That was a great idea, so I did the same.

This went on for awhile, until we tried to get up from the ground and couldn't. In fact, we had to hang onto the grass to keep from falling off. We didn't know what was wrong, and we couldn't stop laughing and being silly. Our legs just wouldn't work right. We got a little scared, too, because we were seeing everything twice.

We didn't know we had found Grandpaw's hard cider barrels. Grandmaw didn't even know about the barrels, since Grandpaw and Grandmaw Jones' farm didn't have any apple trees for cider. It was made by a neighbor who had lots of apple trees and sold hard cider to Grandpaw.

We didn't know what was wrong, until both Grandpaws found us and pronounced us "drunk as skunks." We didn't know what that meant or why we could see two Grandpaws.

He tried every way to roll those cider barrels down the hill into Pipe Creek so Grandmaw wouldn't find them, but they were just too heavy for him to get off the barrel racks.

He even tried draining them out on the ground, but soon he shut off the faucets and said, "By damn, no old-time Civil War veteran alive could do that to good hard cider!"

Giving up, Grandpaw carried us one at a time into the woodshed, where we could sober up out of sight. This good idea fizzled out when Grandmaw came into the shed after some stove wood. She saw us there looking bad.

"Are you poor boys sick?" she asked us gently. "*What is the matter with my two little angels, Grandpaw?*" she yelled at him. Grandpaw must have been too far away by this time to hear her. We were getting sicker, but with Grandmaw's help we slowly crawled on our hands and knees outside, where we heaved up the awful hard cider. Grandmaw put us to bed and gave each of us a big kiss on the forehead. We went right to sleep.

Then Grandmaw got the old splatter gun and went out looking for Grandpaw. When she came back with him, he looked pretty shook up and must have had a lot of explaining to do.

Well, we never did catch the measles, although we both agreed we would have liked a chance to try.

Years later, Grandpaw told Lester and me that after they took us home at noontime the next day, Grandpaw and Grandmaw went out together and found the three oak barrels. They sat down there on the grass by the barrels, tasted a little of the hard cider, and told stories.

In fact, Grandpaw said he drank a lot of the hard cider that day and soon thought he could see a whole row of full hard cider barrels. Feeling generous, he thought he would visit some of the neighbors with Grandmaw and pass those barrels around.

"Then, Grandpaw, what happened?" asked Lester, all caught up in the story.

"Well, boys," Grandpaw said, smiling, "because of that good ol' cider, I just don't recollect nothing else about that beautiful spring afternoon."

|34|

HOMECOMING

One day I was playing with an old tire on the road out in front of our house. I spotted someone down the road a half mile or more away walking toward the house. I ran and told Dad and Mom, since it was unusual to see a person walking rather than riding on a horse or in a wagon.

They ran out to look and didn't stop running. They ran and I ran after them until we had Oscar in our arms. We just stood there for a long time until we could speak.

Oscar hugged us and talked with all the family. He told us that the big long-range guns had been silenced soon after he arrived in the training camps. He spent eighteen months training soldiers to go to the front, but the war ended before he was called to fight on the front lines.

After talking with us for awhile, Oscar went out to see the livestock. He had not seen his prized hogs and cattle for over twenty-one months. He was very happy about how healthy they looked.

Oscar got a bushel basket of ear corn from the corncrib and was walking with it toward the hog pens when suddenly something slammed into his back. Oscar wheeled around and saw that it was one of our big red roosters. He thought it was hungry, so he threw it an ear of corn. The minute he turned around, the old red rooster slammed into his back again.

This made Oscar real angry. He threw ears of corn at the three or four roosters who were now challenging him to a fight. Oscar slammed that whole bushel of corn at the roosters, knocking some of them a stemwinding. But they would just get up and try to torture him again.

Oscar yelled and ran to the house, where Mom was waiting at the door with the twenty-two rifle. She handed it to him, saying, "Go get 'em, doughboy!" We knew we had a big chicken dinner coming up.

Believe me, I was happy to get rid of some of those mean old roosters that had made a champion runner out of me.

Later, Oscar fed his hogs with another basket of corn. Then he went into the livestock barn, where he spotted Arlie Rust pitching horse manure from the stalls and out through an open window.

Oscar went to him and shook his hand.

"Welcome, Arlie," he said, "to our family. Dad told me in a letter that he had hired you. How do you like it here?"

"I never had it so good," Arlie answered. "And I am so glad that you survived the war."

"It was a cinch," said Oscar. "I never saw any direct action, but we will talk about that later."

Oscar left the barn to inspect the rest of his domain and was very pleased with what he saw. He had a big smile on his face.

Oscar was the only person in our neighborhood who went to the big war. When he arrived home, Mom telephoned all the neighbors who knew him, and a big coming-home party raged on for a couple of days. Everyone was smiling, just like Oscar.

|35|

DEAD WORM SMUGGLING

With Oscar home from the war, I turned my thoughts, reluctantly, to going back to school in Metamora.

It was just plain boring in school, so quite often me and my pal Omar Clark would go uptown during the noon hour. We were exploring several buildings that spanned the Old Tow Boat Canal, which ran through Metamora.

Traffic crossed the deep canal on a wide bridge. The railroad depot, a barber shop, a creamery, and two other buildings were built right over it. These buildings were built in a continuous row next to the bridge.

One day we went into the railroad depot, and I went into the old double-hole privy. When I started looking down through the big toilet holes, I saw little fish swimming around near the surface of the deep canal water, so I watched them for awhile. The outside daylight penetrated under the building well enough so that I could see these fish clearly. I figured, if there are little fish, there's got to be big ones down deeper. I knew that big fish liked deep, dark water.

I came out of the two-holer, and Omar was waiting. I said nothing to him about the fish. I only said, "Let's get back to school. The big clock on the depot wall is nearly on one." We ran as fast as we could back to our schoolhouse.

We were ten minutes late. Our teacher said, "You two are penalized ten minutes off your next noon hour."

I could hardly keep my secret. That evening when I got off the school wagon at home, I took a lantern and lit it.

"Harold, where do you think you are going in the dark?" Mom asked.

I hated to lie to Mom, because I had always paid dearly for lying to her before. But how could I explain to her that I wanted to find bait to fish with in an old double-hole privy? My hope was that this time I could pull it off before she could catch on to it.

"I can't wait, Mom," I said. "I gotta go to the outhouse!"

"Hurry, then. Your supper will be ready soon."

I ran with my lantern to the tool shop and got a shovel. I hurried over to a vacant hog pen, where I knew there were lots of fish worms. With my lantern turned down low, I dug like a crazed badger. After a long search, I had stuffed enough worms into my pockets for tomorrow's fishing. I would have put them in a tin can, but I couldn't find one.

I was late and I started running back to the house. I was in such a hurry that I forgot to turn up my lantern light so I could see better. I also took a shortcut through the cow lot.

Somewhere out there I skidded down deep into fresh cow manure. That slowed me down. It was all over me. I slipped into the kitchen, worried about Mom and Dad. When they saw me, they both broke down laughing. They couldn't talk. Oscar and Arlie were hilarious, too.

Lester looked me over slowly. "You *look* like you," he said, "but you *smell* like the back end of a *cow*."

"*I can't stand it!*" said Dollie, holding her nose, and she left the kitchen without her supper.

When Dad got his breath, he said, "It looks like you went to the wrong toilet. Them cows crapped all over you!"

They had so much fun over me that they forgot to question me, or maybe they just thought I had already paid for what I may have done wrong by accidentally swimming in all that cow dung.

The smell was terrible, and the squirming fresh worms in my pockets were getting to me, too.

"I am so dirty," I said to Mom. "Don't you think I should go out to the rain tank and wash?" My new plan was to try to find a can for my worms outside when I washed up at the rain tank. Cans were rare in those days, but I thought I had seen one out there.

"Why, you little darlin', how sweet," she said. "Of course you can, and Lester will go with you to help."

Oh, I didn't like this—my plan had backfired. Ol' Lester got a big bucket, a broom, and a lantern. I was devastated. He threw water all over me and laughed while he broomed me down. He darn-near drowned me with buckets of water. He sure was having fun.

The temperature was cool that night, and I ran fast into the house, nearly frozen. I hurried upstairs and got into some warm, clean clothes that Mom brought up to me. When she left, I grabbed the half-full bed pot from under my bed, and emptied it out the window. It was used only for emergencies when we couldn't make it to the outhouse. I put my squirmy worms into the pot, and replaced it under my bed.

I came down and had supper with the family. I didn't eat much. I was worried about the worms. I couldn't figure out how I could ever get the bed pot out of the house, past Mom and Dad, and on the school wagon the next morning.

The worms in the pot died during the night. Lester didn't know they were in it, and he drowned them all.

I already had so many problems behind me, that I was

determined to get the dead worms to the depot come hell or high horseweeds.

My first challenge the next morning was to control myself when I saw what Lester had done to my worms. Boy oh boy, was I ever upset! Then I had to figure out a way to get the worms out of the bed pot. In a dresser drawer I found one of Mom's long hat pins. I locked the bedroom door so Lester wouldn't crash in on me, and started spearing the dead worms one by one with Mom's hat pin. Finally I had most of them.

But the biggest problem still remained. How could I get them past everybody in the whole family?

Now dressed in my clean clothes, I desperately decided my only hope was to put the dead worms into my pockets. I hurried downstairs for breakfast.

"Well," said Dad, smiling, "it looks like you are all cleaned up and ready for school." He didn't know the half of it. I was also ready to go fishing!

I ate my breakfast, grabbed my lunch bucket, and pulled myself up on the school wagon. Me and Lester were the first kids on. One mile later, four more kids got on. I stayed at the back of the wagon by the door, because my bait-loaded pockets were starting to smell.

I thought if I could make it three more miles to the shortcut through the woods, I could get my worms to school without dying of the smell. When the wagon reached the shortcut, I jumped out carrying my dinner bucket and headed down the trail. Then I looked back and saw seven boys, including Lester, following me. I thought they knew something about my dead bait, but as it turned out, they just wanted to walk the old road with me.

We made it to the main road in time to get back on the school wagon for the last stretch. I got off again and walked the last quarter mile in the fresh air to school. I was so close to my goal, I couldn't afford to lose now.

I had fifteen minutes before class, and a tin can just seemed to be waiting for me in the school's woodshed. I took the dead worms, now almost rotten from wear and tear in my pockets, and put them into this precious can along with some fishing line and three hooks that I had brought. I hid it all under some coal and hurried into my classroom.

Omar and I sat together in a double seat. He started whispering to me about the kid sitting ahead of us and how he smelled so bad. Omar wondered what he had for breakfast that made him stink so.

Omar was from a high-class family and was a very likable kid. I figured right then that I could not invite him to fish with me through the depot toilet holes during the fifty-minute noon hour. I didn't want him to know that I was the kid who was stinking up the classroom. Once he got a whiff of my smelly bait, he would know it was me.

Soon I weakened, however, and let him in on my whole plan. It turned out that Omar liked the idea of fishing in the depot's privy.

We sat quietly for ten minutes into our noon hour, then grabbed our lunch buckets and raced off for the woodshed to get my bait can.

|36|

FISHING IN A TWO-HOLER

We ran uptown as fast as we could. When we got to the railroad depot we casually entered the two-holer and locked the door so no one could bother us.

"Do you think they'll bite on those rotten worms?" Omar asked.

"My Dad said that the big catfish really go for dead worms," I said. Then I thought to myself, "But he didn't say anything about *rotten* dead worms."

"Omar," I said out loud again, "I remember Dad used dead worms in Pipe Creek last summer, and he got a nice big catfish. That is why I have hung on to these old, dead, rotten fish worms, no matter how much trouble it is causing me." Omar nodded, accepting what I said without question.

I had enough line and hooks for both Omar and me. We baited up just as a passenger train pulled into the station from Cincinnati heading north to Indianapolis. The train let off a few passengers while it took on water. By this time, Omar and I were both fishing like mad and hoping we would have no more problems.

Omar had never fished at all before. Suddenly he had a big one on his hook! The fishing line was stout and sure to hold the fish. Omar was scared and also thrilled. The big fish came up to where he could see us and we could see him. It was a giant blue catfish. It must have weighed fifteen pounds or more. I pulled in my line from the second hole so as not to tangle up with Omar's big fish.

Suddenly a knock came at our door. We looked at each other, scared. A man said nervously, "Let me in—I have got to use the toilet!" We decided to ignore the man and together we landed the big fish. I grabbed hold of his gills on each side to help pull him, wiggling wildly, up through the toilet hole. Wet and excited, we laid him out on the floor and he took up nearly all of the foot room.

The man outside our door was threatening to get the manager, so we finally let him in. He was a tall, well-dressed stranger. He saw the giant fish on the floor and heard us talking.

"Mind if I try my luck in *that* hole, boys," he asked, "while I am sitting on *this* hole?"

He became as enthusiastic about our big fish as we were. After awhile he got a nice bite and hooked it. We could hear the train pulling out, and now somebody else was knocking on the door. The stranger fishing with us jumped to his feet and landed a big channel catfish, with his pants still around his ankles.

The knocking on the door stopped. I guess they must have gotten scared off by all of the excitement going on inside.

Finally the stranger said, "I have to go now, boys. Maybe we can do this again, sometime. Oh, and by the way, you can keep my nice big fish." We never saw that man again. I have often wondered what he thought about fishing in a two-holer, and whether he missed his train in order to catch the giant catfish.

We smuggled the two big fish out and hurried across the street to the icehouse, where they put them on ice for us until evening.

"Where did you boys get the two big fish?" asked the ice-house man. He knew Omar and me and our folks.

"We will let you know later," I said, "because we are late for school again. We were penalized ten minutes for being late yesterday." And off we ran.

We ran back to school like two scared turkeys on the day before Thanksgiving, only to find class had already taken up. We walked in quietly and tried to sit down without being seen.

"Harold and Omar, stand up!" our teacher said. We did. "You two are penalized *thirty* minutes off your noon hour to-morrow, and if you two are tardy again, I am going to take the whole noon hour away from you."

We were almost never late again, since we were afraid she would tell our folks, but we fished in the depot privy holes several times after that. We were proud to take fish home to show off and to help grace the supper table. Maybe even our dads suffered with envy. But it was an awful lot of trouble to get the big fish home, a half at a time, without telling exactly where they came from.

Then, somehow, our secret got out. Soon all the kids from school were lined up at the depot's double-hole fishing spot, pretending to be kids needing to use the toilet.

At this point, the manager saw that something had to be done. He said, "You kids are interfering too much with the paying passengers. From now on, all of you must use the toilet at your school. And if you don't have a toilet at school, I will personally contact the proper authorities."

Lester, Omar, and me went back to the depot several days later to try our luck again. Lester had everything he needed to fish with in his pockets. Then we discovered that the privy door was padlocked.

So while Omar and I pretended to look at some train pictures, Lester went into the office and asked for the key. The manager had never seen Lester before and gave him the key.

Lester was in the privy about twenty minutes by the wall clock. He had the door locked inside and was fishing like mad. He came out fast with his big fish hidden but wiggling wildly inside his coat.

The three of us ran laughing all the way back to school, but once again we were late. Me and Omar got penalized all of the next noon hour and had to write one hundred times, "I will not be late again for class."

Slick Ol' Lester, however, got off scot-free by giving our teacher his big catfish. Lester was a very generous person, and he was always giving something away. He did this his whole life.

|37|

MY AWFUL KID CRIME

During the winter, some of us kids practiced our ice skating on Duck Creek at the edge of the school yard. Duck Creek flowed past the school and then went on through Metamora for about one mile. It moved into a viaduct under the Old Tow Boat Canal and emptied out into the Whitewater River.

When the ice started breaking up in the early spring, I wore my new rubber boots and waded out into Duck Creek. I discovered that I could ride on large ice cakes down the swift, deep waters. I had a great time impressing all the girls with my riding. Sometimes I would have a hard time getting off the ice without getting soaked, and the girls, including my "secret" girlfriend, Crystal Schankel, would do a lot of squealing—this I really loved!

One of the Jackson twins wanted me to put him on a big ice cake. He got on my back and I carried him out to a nice large one. He got off onto the ice and was looking great as he floated off down Duck Creek.

"Let me know when you want off," I said to him. He never did. He was happy to see some of the girls watching him. He didn't notice that he was getting farther out into swifter and deeper water.

Soon after that big favor I did for him, the school bell rang out to let us know the noon hour was over.

My teacher was still penalizing me by taking away my whole noon hour if I was just a little late now. So I ran like a cockroach with his fuse lit for the classroom, leaving the Jackson twin alone on the ice cake.

We were all settling down to our studies when our teacher noticed that one of the twins was missing. She said, "When he comes in, he will be penalized four times the time he is tardy."

Well, he never showed up, and the rest of the afternoon was very long for me. A search party was organized, and a search of the creek and its banks was made. When they worked their way down to the Old Tow Boat Canal viaduct, they finally found him.

He was standing on an ice ledge, holding onto a large ten-foot icicle that was hanging down from the top of the old canal viaduct into Duck Creek. He was nearly frozen but was safely rescued. He was back in school the next day.

The threat our teacher had made about penalizing him was never brought up. Everyone asked him how he got down there, a whole mile away from school and out on an ice ledge. He answered, "I got on a large ice cake at the school grounds and had an exciting ride down Duck Creek. When it passed under the old canal viaduct, I jumped from the ice cake to the ice ledge, where I was rescued."

All through his testimony, I was in a state of frozen terror. I knew that if he told the truth, I would be barred from school for the duration and maybe from Indiana forever.

I will never forget how gallantly that Jackson twin protected me when he could have had my scalp for that awful kid crime. Even the girls didn't tell on me, and I think I was in love with *all* of them. If any of the boys gave my girl friends a bad time, I fought like mad to protect them

|38|

THE KING OF METAMORA

The Jackson twins lived right in Metamora, and their folks owned and ran Jackson's General Store. All the school kids loved to go into their store because their Mom and Dad were always so thoughtful. If I had only a penny to spend, Mr. Jackson would cut down the price of almost any item so I could buy it. For older folks he would cut one cent worth of chewing tobacco from a standard nickel plug if that was all they could afford. He would open a pack of anything. Kids could buy four to six pieces of candy for a penny, and adults could buy two cigarettes from a pack for a penny. The Jacksons knew most of us kids by name, and they knew our folks, too.

Believe it or not, this system helped the Jacksons stay in business and made it possible for even the poorest kids to buy something with only a penny. Of course, the Jacksons also had big money items of all kinds for sale. It was a well-stocked store.

Dan Currie's garage and gas service was another place my folks visited. Whether you needed one gallon or five gallons of gas, Mr. Currie would carry it out to your car in a can and pour the gas into your car's tank using a funnel. The gas pump hadn't been invented yet. What a hard job that must have been for Mr. Currie.

Also in Metamora there was a livery barn. We loved to climb up into the haymow and eat our school lunches from our lunch buckets there. We also liked to stand and watch the blacksmith in his shop, shoeing horses with handmade horseshoes.

We had one doctor in town, Doctor Cupp. There was also a drugstore, a library, and two hotels. One of the hotels was owned by the Ratz family. Their daughter, Vivian Ratz, was in my class at school.

There was a flour mill driven by water power from the Old Tow Boat Canal. My folks took lots of wheat and corn there to have it made into flour and cornmeal. This mill in Metamora is still in use today, and tourists are able to buy stone-ground cornmeal and flour.

A sawmill adjoined our school on one side with only a fence between our play yard and the log pile at the mill. The mill was powered by a big steam engine.

Dad and Oscar belonged to the Damon and Pythias Lodge. Dad also served on the Metamora Township Advisory Board. Lots of times I would sit out in the old Maxwell at night, waiting for them to get out from one of their meetings. There was another lodge in Metamora, called the Red Man Lodge.

In addition to the Jackson General Store, there was another general store in our town. It was owned and operated by L. Martindale and Steve Jenks. This store was much larger than the Jackson's store. It carried expensive items and a better line of merchandise. They even had a jewelry shop in the back. This was where Mom did most of her shopping. They knew my Mom and Dad and all of the Hannebaum kids.

I often went into this store with Mom and watched her shop for lots of things. Mr. Martindale would ring everything up, Mom would sign a receipt, and we would carry out our bags of merchandise. I never saw any money used to pay for these items.

One day at the noon hour, I went into the Martindale store, told them what I wanted, and simply signed my name for it. I thought this was great—I didn't need any money and could have anything I wanted.

I started acting like the King of Metamora! I got lots of goodies by signing. Life was really wonderful, until the end of the month when my folks received their statement from the Martindale General Store!

After looking over the statement, Mom and Dad sat me down. I sure had lots and lots of explaining to do! I tried to tell Mom and Dad that you just didn't *need* money in the Martindale's store, like you did at the Jackson's store. This got me into even more trouble. I thought they were going to kill me this time for sure.

After that I never signed my name for any kind of merchandise. I learned a lesson then that I have carried through life. If I didn't have the cash to pay for what I wanted, I didn't buy it until I did. This rule even went for all the new cars I bought, my farm in later years, and all the houses I have owned throughout my lifetime, so I have never been in financial debt in my adult life.

|39|

BURIED GOLD

The year was 1918, and I was eight years old. These were ordinary times for most people, but that year something far from ordinary happened to me.

This is a true story about something that probably no other eight-year-old on our Earth ever experienced. Even now, more than seventy years later, I have vivid memories daily that take me back to a small plot of ground under a dogwood tree about three miles from Metamora, Indiana.

It began one spring morning when me and Lester and Bert climbed on the school wagon. Arlie Rust was driving the team of horses toward our school in Metamora that day. It was a normal start for what looked to be an unexceptional day.

We slowly rode one mile up Pipe Creek, where three more kids got aboard. One of these kids was a boy named Evo—pronounced "Eev'l"—Shekel. Evo was a muscular eleven-year-old boy with a stormy disposition. He had been adopted by Cord and Alice Shekel along with a girl named Lena. Evo's nationality was Russian Baltoslavic. They were all living with Cord's mother, a wealthy lady. I liked Grandmother Shekel a lot. She owned a large farm, and their farmhouse was a twenty-room mansion.

Evo had been a pal of ours for the last two years, but me and Lester didn't dare say the wrong thing to him or we would have a fight on our hands. I was always afraid of him because he was three times my size. Lester, however, was closer to Evo's age and size, and was always ready for a good fight. I must say here that I have never seen or been in a "good fight." My Dad often said, "When you are in a fight, always use your head." Well, I tried that once and damn-near got it pulverized. Dad saw me afterwards and commented, "It looks like you tried to use your head all right, Harold, but your nose and chin got in the way."

Although Lester and Evo were just kids, they would often fight until one or the other could take no more and then both would collapse from exhaustion. When they finally got back on their feet, they would stroll off with their arms around each other as if nothing had happened.

This particular morning when Evo got on the school wagon, I noticed he was holding his overalls up with both hands. He was trying to take the weight off his suspenders because they were cutting into his shoulders. Brave and foolhardy I asked, "Evo, why are you holding up your pants?" He put his fist against my nose and growled, "None of your damn business."

As the school wagon moved slowly along, Lester and Evo jumped off the wagon and headed down the shortcut trail that ran toward Metamora through the woods. Bert stayed on, but I followed them.

About a half mile into the woods, Evo said, "Let's stop here." He looked around then added, "I got something I want to show you two. It is awful important."

Lester and me joined around him and Lester looked at me and said, "Now don't ask me what *important* means, 'cause at your age you are supposed to know." I didn't ask any questions, but I thought to myself that maybe *important* meant *something heavy* because, as we walked along, Evo still held up his heavy pants by hooking his thumbs under his suspenders.

He didn't show us anything, but started to walk again. He led us about halfway down a wooded ravine, where the trail seemed to be squeezed by the weight of the big hillside. Without thinking much, I asked Evo, "Can I help you hold up your pants?"

He hit me in the stomach, knocking the wind from me. He walked on for five or six steps and then came back. As I lay writhing in the dirt, he said, "Don't get up yet, because I may hit you again." I stayed down there for a few more minutes, even though he walked down the hill. I was dreaming of the day when I might be big enough to kill him.

Then I heard a commotion down the hill and saw good Ol' Lester beating the hell out of Evo because he had hit me in the belly. Evo seemed a little slowed down and awkward, probably because of his heavy pants. They fought as usual until they could fight no more, then they disappeared. Lester's fighting for me made me love Lester beyond all explaining.

I got up and staggered after them down to the bottom of the hill. There I had to stop and do nothing but look at the beautiful flowering woods and at the hundreds of birds of all colors and varieties that were singing. The sound they were making was deafening in a very pleasant way.

I got to a place where I could look far down the trail and was not surprised to see Evo and Lester arm-in-arm as if nothing had happened. Still, this sight almost caused me to gag.

I yelled to them, and about two hundred yards farther, they finally sat down and waited for me. I ran and when I reached them, Evo said, "We have only one hour left to catch the school wagon at the other end of the trail."

"If we miss the school wagon," Lester said, "we will be late for school."

I knew what that meant. "That means no noon hour for me for sure, and maybe the same for you two," I said.

Evo got up and told Lester to get up. We were standing around him again, and he seemed to make a decision.

"I got something for you two," he said. "Hold out your double hands, so I can fill them with money." He looked at me and said, "Don't you *dare* tell anybody."

Evo took gold coins from his pockets by the handfuls and put them into my double hands, heaping them up full. He then did the same for Lester, filling his double hands full. Evo kept about a third of the coins. The three of us stood carefully looking at all the gold coins in our hands.

"What are they?" I soon asked. I had never seen anything like it before. The money that I was used to didn't look like this. "They sure are pretty," I added, looking at them more closely.

Evo seemed to get very nervous whenever I said anything.

"*Shut up!*" he shouted. "Just get rid of it—bury it—or hide it somewhere! *Now get lost!*"

I slowly turned to go without taking my eyes off the heavy coins in my hands. I said, "Where did you get them?" I should have known better. He kicked my backside hard and shouted, "*Get lost!*"

I quickly stuffed all of my gold into my pockets and picked up several coins I had dropped. I stumbled through the heavy undergrowth at the creek bank and found my way into the woods.

I was very scared, but I could not tell myself why. I was doing some awful hard thinking, and it felt like my brain was sweating. Was it stolen by him? If so, would Lester and me get into trouble? Where did he get it? Should I tell Mom and Dad? Then I remembered Evo saying, "Don't you dare tell anyone! Just get rid of it—bury it—or hide it somewhere! *Now get lost!*"

I hurried along the creek, then climbed up the hill a ways. I sat down and looked around. I could see no one. I dug a hole with my bare hands under a crooked dogwood tree. It was easy going through the first four inches of black top soil, then much harder digging into about eight more inches of soggy yellow clay. This was the kind of clay that made good marbles. I measured the depth with a stick—it was about one foot deep.

I placed all of the gold into the bottom of the hole, then pushed it down tightly. Next I gathered all the yellow clay and put it on top of the gold. Last I pushed in the black top soil and packed it down tightly. I used a tree branch to brush old leaves over it to make it look natural-like, just like the surroundings.

Without that crooked dogwood tree, I could not have found the hiding place of the gold even the next day. I took one more look around, then hurried back to the old shortcut trail. No one else was around. I thought Lester and Evo must have gone on down the trail to catch the school wagon, so I turned on my Olympic champion speed and ran hard and fast to catch up with them. I rounded a curve in the trail where I could see a long ways ahead, but saw no one. I was scared that I would miss the school wagon, but despite my better judgment, I turned back to see if I had missed them. I thought I might be able to find tracks made by them. As I ran back around the same curve, I spotted them coming, and stopped to catch my breath while I waited.

"What did you do with *your* gold money?" I excitedly asked Evo.

"*Shut up! None of your damn business!*" he shouted at me. "*I buried it,*" he added in a mean way.

We hurried on down the trail in silence, arriving at the main road just in time to see the school wagon coming.

While we waited for the wagon to get up to us, Evo asked me, "What did you do with your gold coins?"

Suddenly I decided not to get on the school wagon, and instead I ran like a turpentined coyote and hollered back, "*It's none of your damn business!*"

|40|

CONFESSION—AND LOST TREASURE

Everything was normal that day at school, except for Lester. He was one of the "big shots" of all time at school, anyway, and now he was planning a giveaway party that would make him look like a god to the rest of the kids.

At noon that day, Lester went uptown. With a gold coin or two that he didn't bury, he bought twenty pounds of hard candy for all the kids. He also bought a big box of chocolates for his teacher. To top it off, he bought a ruby ring and a diamond ring for his two girlfriends at school.

The rings were beautiful and his two girlfriends liked them a lot, but they were too big for the fingers of ten-year-old girls. So Lester put them back into his pocket, and later on put them on his own bigger fingers. He also bought an expensive gold Elgin railroad watch with an elegant gold chain and fob, which he wore on the front of his faded overalls. He had a fortune's worth of fine jewelry on a ten-cent pair of overalls.

Lester even made a soapbox speech that afternoon to all of us kids on the evils of being rich. He had so many friends that day, that all the kids in his class ignored their teacher. Our town's brick school had three large rooms with a teacher in each room, and they were all having trouble keeping the attention of their students. I don't know what the teachers thought.

Well, Lester, Evo, and me didn't—couldn't—imagine the hell that would be unleashed on us when we got home. We arrived long after dark. It was stormy weather in more ways than one. We quietly sneaked into the house and headed for the big kitchen. Mom's sharp eye caught a flash from the diamond ring that Lester was wearing. Mom reached out and caught his hand.

"Lester," she said sharply. "Where did you get this?" Mom knew good jewelry. Poor Lester dropped his head, then answered weakly, "I can't tell." He received a sharp slap to his face, and it helped him remember that truth is necessary and must be given to mothers.

Lester, not being responsible, told Mom the whole story of how Evo gave each of us lots of gold coins. While it thundered outside he explained how he and Evo had buried gold coins on the hillside in the woods that same morning. Lester also said he knew where I had buried mine. I knew that he knew of no such thing.

Mom's good nature was faltering fast and she became angrier and more frustrated. She called for Dad, then got on the phone and called the Cord Shekel's residence. They knew nothing over there about the theft of the gold coins or Evo doing anything wrong or that he had given anything to Lester and me.

When Mom and Dad saw the fine gold Elgin railroad watch and the diamond and ruby rings, they were in a state of ferocity and immediately took all the jewelry away from Lester.

Before long we could hear the rumbling of the Shekel carriage and the hoofbeats of their running horses as they galloped in the rain up to the hitch racks in our backyard.

My folks and the Shekels were very close friends and neighbors. There was a loud and distinct knock, and when Dad opened the door the Shekels entered without speaking. Mr. Cord Shekel was a large, powerful yet gentle man, but he came in dragging tough Evo by the nape of his neck. Mom held a lantern outside on that rainy night for the rest of the Shekel family, including Evo's sister Lena, to see to come on in.

Mr. Shekel, still holding Evo in the middle of the room, thundered, "Evo, you tell Mr. and Mrs. Hannebaum *exactly* what you told me at home!" But Evo kept a stone face and would say nothing. Mr. Shekel repeated his demand, but Evo stubbornly still said nothing.

Cord Shekel's patience failed him and his even temper broke down. He was a powerful man and believed and practiced self-discipline, but at this point he threw all control to the wind and his temper flared. He threw Evo to the floor and placed his large boot against the boy's throat.

"*Do as I say!*" Mr. Shekel roared. "*Talk or I will choke you to death!*" He put even more pressure on Evo's throat, but of course, Evo's face just turned blue from being choked, and he could not say anything. Dad jumped to Mr. Shekel's side and put his hand gently on the angry man's arm.

"Let up on the pressure with your foot," Dad said, "so he can get his breath, *then* maybe he will be willing to talk."

Mr. Shekel removed his foot, and Evo was able to gasp in some breath. Then the boy started talking.

"I 'ram-sacked' the entire upstairs ten rooms," he began hoarsely. We knew these were the rooms where Grandmother Shekel lived. She never allowed anyone up there, not even her son, Cord, or his wife, Alice.

"I found lots of gold coins," Evo continued, rubbing his throat. "They were hidden under the plush carpeting. There was a lot more there than I could carry. I could see Grandmother working in her flower garden from the upstairs window. I knew that I could leave by the upstairs fire escape if Grandmother left the garden."

We all stood there frozen, listening. It was so unbelievable that their adopted son could and would do a thing like that.

"I got out of there with all the gold coins that I could carry," Evo continued. "It was almost too heavy for my pockets. I knew I couldn't take them all to school, so I got off the school wagon at the shortcut trail. Lester and Harold jumped off, too. I wasn't going to tell them, but then I decided to give some to Lester and some to Harold. I told them to bury it all somewhere in the woods."

Grandmother Shekel was now so upset that she was shaking like a leaf in a windstorm.

"We will have to go look now," she cried, "and get my precious gold coins before these wicked thieves forget where they buried them!" When she said *wicked thieves* she was including, of course, Lester and me, putting us on the same level with Evo. I just couldn't believe those words coming from my dear old lady friend that I thought so much of.

It was really raining outside now, and Mom said, "Lester can go with Evo, Oscar, John, and Cord to look for the gold coins, but Harold can't go out at all on a night like this because of his rheumatoid arthritis." I was happy to hear that I was excused. After some thought, Mom added, "Harold may go out into the woods some weekend when it is not raining to get the gold he buried." Alice and Grandmother Shekel nodded their heads in agreement.

"I'll get Harold's gold tonight," Lester told them. "I know where he buried it." When I heard that, I knew Lester was thinking about my well-being and was covering for me. He had no idea where I had buried the gold. I don't think that even I could have found it on that dark night in a raging storm. But Mom had already put her foot down, and that was law. I was sent upstairs to bed without my supper.

The ladies stayed with Mom while the men went with Evo and Lester. Carrying lanterns, they set off on a three-mile trek along the shortcut trail through the rain-soaked woods and hills in search of Grandmother Shekel's precious gold coins.

Had they followed the main road, it would have been a five-mile trip. The shortcut reduced the distance, but the trail was awful dangerous as the three creeks, normally small, were now torrential rivers because of this downpour. In places these streams would swim a horse. Lester and Evo, as big as they were, had to be helped across several times.

In the early morning hours, the search party returned

and woke us all up. They had found Evo's and Lester's buried gold. It made Grandmother Shekel very happy to get so many of her gold coins back.

Mom made hot coffee for the cold, tired and wet fellows. Later she put on a big breakfast for the whole crowd. Everybody seemed to be in good spirits again, but Evo looked like hell. I bet with myself that he would never again go upstairs into Grandmother Shekel's part of their mansion.

As they were leaving that morning, Mom again reassured the Shekels that I could go out on a nice warm afternoon during some weekend and get what was left of the gold.

"That is fine," said Grandmother Shekel. "These gold coins were minted in the early 1800s in England, that is why they are so very precious." We all nodded in agreement with her. Even in that day, they were worth a great deal more than their face value, and we knew that the value of these coins would someday be worth a king's fortune.

Lester and I were never again allowed to get off the school wagon to walk the shortcut. Mom took all of Lester's fine jewelry back to Martindale's General Store and received the gold coins back. She paid for all of the hard candy and chocolates that couldn't be returned.

Mom told all of the store owners in Metamora not to sell anything to her kids without a written note from her. This sure wrecked our fun of being big shots with our classmates.

As time went on, everyone was very busy. Bert finished school and the gold was forgotten. I was glad of that. I hated all the trouble it had caused. I was now scared to even look at that shortcut we used to walk. The Shekels never did say a word about it again.

Many decades later, I returned to Indiana to look for the gold, but things had changed to the point that I couldn't find it.

And now, there is lost gold somewhere still in the hills of Southern Indiana.

|41|

DR. JONES GOES CRAZY

Mom's brother, Lucius Tobias Jones, was a Navy medical corpsman during World War I. We hadn't seen him for a long time, until he came to our home on a well-deserved forty-day leave.

Mom offered him a downstairs bedroom. He replied, "It is unhealthy to sleep indoors, unless one *has* to." We were a little startled.

"I will make my bed," he continued, "on the hard wood floor of the hay wagon out by the barn, if that is all right with you and John." Mom and Dad agreed.

Dad stayed up until three in the morning with Uncle Lucius, who we now called "Doc," to listen to his war stories. Mom wouldn't let Lester and me hear. "But Mom," we pleaded, "we want to hear his stories *bad*." Mom replied, "That is just what they are—*bad*—for little boys."

Lummox kept us all awake from three o'clock on by barking at Uncle Doc. I guess the old dog figured something was wrong with him, because nobody ever sleeps on the floor of a hay wagon.

What a long night that was. I was upset first from not being allowed to stay up, and second from not being able to sleep because of ol' Lummox. Then at early daylight I heard Uncle Doc laughing awful hard and loud outside. I got out of bed and ran out to the hay wagon to see what was so funny. I stood there and watched as my uncle lay in his bed laughing hard at the fading moon—or maybe at just nothing.

I hurried back to the kitchen where Mom was fixing breakfast and told her. She said, "Don't pay any attention to him. He is so happy to be home from the Navy that he can't keep from laughing."

Pretty soon the loud laughing stopped, but then I was startled to hear a crash. I ran outside and back to the hay wagon, and watched in amazement while Uncle Doc stood straight up on the solid wooden floor of the hay wagon, held his head back and his hands behind him, and then fell forward on his chest and face. It sounded like his two hundred and forty pounds were going to go right through the floor of the wagon.

That really scared me and Lummox. We thought Uncle Doc had gone mad during the night. Maybe Mom was right and it was the delight of being home, but I felt it was definitely dangerous.

I ran back and reported to Mom again. "He is plumb crazy," I said. "Should we take him to a doctor?"

"But he *is* a doctor," Mom replied.

"Mom, he is too crazy to doctor himself," I said. Mom, with a smile on her face, said, "Let's wait until he comes in for breakfast, and we will both have a talk with him."

Shortly after, when Uncle Doc strode in and sat down at our kitchen table, Mom told him about my concerns.

"Don't you worry about your old Uncle Doc, Harold," he said. "I was just taking my exercises. The laughing exercise was to stimulate and loosen up my throat and stomach muscles. It also vigorously exercises my lungs. You see, when you are asleep all night, some of these organs and muscles tend to become slightly dormant, which means *too relaxed*, and they do not respond to your needs readily."

Thanks to Lummox, none of my muscles had been too relaxed from sleeping through the past night, but I said nothing.

Uncle Doc leaned back in his chair, smiled, and said, "Now, about me falling on my chest and face, well, that is a very hard exercise to do, and must be first practiced a lot on a soft object, like a mattress or feather bed." He stood up to point to his various muscles. "When the art is mastered, it is very good for your back, chest, and neck muscles, but don't ever have your hands *tied* behind you for this exercise. Always hold them free, so if something goes wrong, you can catch yourself with your hands and not get hurt."

He didn't have to worry about me ever tying my hands behind my back and then trying to fall on *my* face! But these exercises Uncle Doc did down through his life must have been good for him. He died a natural death at the age of ninety-five.

In the Navy, Uncle Doc apparently learned a lot about using stilts. I thought he probably used them during battle, so the enemy would undershoot him, or maybe so he could wade to shore if his ship sank. On several occasions I watched him get out of an upstairs window and walk away on stilts that he had leaned up against the house.

One day he got off the house roof onto his stilts and walked around the yard. Ol' Lummox playfully grabbed the bottom of one of the stilts and pulled it out from under him, and Uncle Doc took a nasty fall. He was not hurt, however, probably because he was an expert at falling and at laughing.

TRIP TO THE WILD WEST

Doc Jones became itchy to go someplace before his Navy leave ran out. He decided he might enjoy a visit to one of his brothers, Scott Jones, who was living in Idaho with his new wife, Ella. Scott, a carpenter by trade, was helping to build the town of Milner, Idaho, and the new Milner Dam on the wild Snake River.

Uncle Doc bought a brand new Hupmobile Sport Roadster. He said to Mom, "Let's take a trip to Idaho. We can surprise Scott and Ella." Mom jumped at the chance.

"But what will I do with my kids?" she asked.

"I will talk to your housekeeper, Mrs. Milbourne, to see if she would be willing to take on this added job for a little more money," Doc answered.

Mrs. Milbourne agreed to take care of the kids, and Mom asked Dad about going to Idaho with her brother.

"Go ahead and take the trip," Dad answered. "I need the rest." He knew he couldn't stop her anyway.

I cried when I found out that Mom was going clear out to Idaho with Uncle Doc. I couldn't help it. I knew there were lots of Indians and tons of bears in that wild country. They just laughed at my concerns.

When they started to study what lay ahead of them, they discovered that the unfinished Lincoln Highway was two thousand miles of rocks, dirt, mud, dust, and gravel, with very few straightaways. Doc asked around for more information.

"In some places," Doc reported back to us, "they say that the construction boys got confused and the road actually heads back to Indiana."

Mom kept a diary of this trip, and I have heard some of the stories over and over, so I can tell you a lot of what happened on their adventure into the wild West.

They camped out nearly every night in a small two-room wall tent and cooked over an open campfire. They did eat a few times in restaurants and stayed a few nights in hotels, because the outdoor life was awful grueling for them.

They saw real cowboys and real Indians many times. When possible, they even camped with the Indians or with the cowboys, for safety reasons.

Rattlesnakes were plentiful and water was very scarce. They had to carry a thirty-gallon container of water at all times. Flat tires and overheated radiators were a way of life.

In those days if an automobile was traveling very far, it was a normal thing to see four or five tires on rims strapped to the back of the car, each tire carrying seventy-five pounds of air.

Toward the end of their first long day of travel, Uncle Doc and Mom and the Hupmobile crossed the Mississippi River on a ferryboat for a toll of fifteen cents.

"Think, Flora, of all the money they are making here in a day. Probably as much as fifty or sixty cents in a whole day, with hardly enough work to do to keep them awake," Doc said.

By the second night they reached Kansas, where the leader of a small Indian tribe gave Mom some cleaned prairie-chicken meat for their supper. He helped Mom cook the chicken and cooked sourdough in her Dutch oven, then stayed and ate with them. He posted four Indians to guard her tent in return for the good supper he had.

The next morning, the third day of their trip, more than one hundred Indians helped them pack, with lots of solemn, well-behaved Indian kids watching. "Hold it, Doc," Mom said as they were about to drive off. "We gotta do something to give those little kids smiling faces."

Mom located a well-filled burlap bag and dug out one of several large sacks of store-bought hard candy, and another one full of homemade candy. She gave five pieces of candy to each little Indian kid.

"That is probably the happiest tribe west of the Mississippi River today," she said, smiling as they drove away.

Early in the evening they saw a range fire about twenty miles ahead, fed by brush, dry bunch grass, and wind. They stopped and made camp early to avoid the fire.

The next morning the fire was still raging southeast of where they were. They drove through miles and miles of blackened land, all burned over and barren.

"I am so glad the fire veered to the south," said Mom, "so that it missed the Indian camp."

In the afternoon, when they rounded a rock outcropping, another Indian camp appeared. It was located in a beautiful valley with a creek and lots of trees, something not often seen in Kansas.

The Indians were, as usual, cautious but friendly. They offered fresh fish and a welcome to stay awhile. Mom took the fish, since she felt they must not turn down their gifts. Only three of the Indians in this tribe could speak and understand English. Mom and Doc gave them some hard candy. They also gave the Indians black gunpowder to use in their two ancient muskets.

Doc was particularly interested in their guns. He also owned a muzzle-loader musket, but he used his only for fun shooting. The Indians told them that they used the weapons for hunting, although they had no bullets anymore.

"We are good at getting wild game with our big musket rifles without using lead balls," one of the Indians told them. Doc couldn't understand what they were saying, and he asked them to explain.

"We shoot straight hardwood rods instead. We start out with straight dried hickory or hard maple sticks about a foot and a half long. Anything smaller just bounces off. Then we whittle them and sand them until they fit tightly into the rifle barrel. Each one can be used over many times, until they are lost or shattered by hitting rocks."

The Indians showed them one of their wooden ramrod bullets that was still in very good shape, although it had been used many times. "We invented this ramrod bullet a long time ago when we ran out of lead balls. We needed to continue hunting," they said.

Mom and Uncle Doc were impressed with the frontier resourcefulness of these proud people.

Then Doc turned his attention back to their trip. "How far is it from here to Idaho?" he asked them.

"About one and a half moons by horseback," one answered him. Doc scratched his head and did some figuring, but he could not translate that correctly for automobile travel.

Mom and Doc camped at the edge of the creek that evening. There was no bridge, so they carefully inspected the place where they would have to cross in the morning. It seemed to be okay for a horse, but the water was too deep for the Hupmobile.

There were a lot of big rocks on the creek banks, so Mom and Uncle Doc started to shove them into the water. Two Indian boys looked on for awhile, then raced up the hill to their camp.

Suddenly down the hill came forty big Indians. Mom and Doc were worried that they might have offended them, but one of the braves who spoke English said, "A flash flood washed out this crossing a few days ago. You are the first ones to come by after the washout." The Indians swarmed down and got busy putting rocks neatly into place until the creek water was running through them.

Doc started up the new Hupmobile and drove it across, with about forty Indians almost carrying the automobile to the other side. Doc, being a generous man, had to give them something. He knew that he and Mom probably would have had to turn back without these wonderful and helpful people.

"All I have," he told Mom, "is a box of cigars and one full quart bottle of whiskey."

Doc gave them these gifts, and the chief and his people were very happy. The next morning, on their fifth day on the road, some of the Indians rode their horses beside the Hupmobile for several hours, just to make sure that they had help if they needed it. Finally, the horse riders could no longer keep up, and they turned around with a friendly wave.

That evening they made camp in the foothill country of Nebraska. They arrived after dark at an old deserted homestead among some aspen trees. They had to break out the kerosene lantern to see, and they ate most of their supper cold, but they fried their salted-down fresh fish in a frying pan over a campfire. In those days, there were no camp stoves.

They found that it was very easy to sleep on their trip, because it was so tiring to ride in the car. It was not the fault of the car—it was simply the rough roads that made driving difficult. Rough roads also meant lots of flat tires, and it was tiring to patch and change so many tires.

The next day they drove all day in the rain with the car top up, then came to the little town of Scotts Bluff, Nebraska, where they found a restaurant and a hotel.

"I thought it was heaven," Mom said, "to find a big tub of hot water to bathe in, a clean pillow to lay my head on, and clean white sheets to sleep under."

On the seventh morning of their trip, after a wonderful breakfast in the restaurant, she told her brother, "I have decided to stay here. Please pick me up on your way back from Idaho."

"I like it here, too," said Doc, teasing her back. "I like it here more than any place I've ever been, and I don't plan to go any further. Of course, I'll help you figure out some way to get home to Indiana."

Back on the road again, they felt pretty good. As they had crossed Nebraska, they counted only four cars and two wagons, but they saw many horseback riders. Mom and Doc were thankful that they were so close to Idaho now, with only Wyoming and the Continental Divide a short distance ahead of them.

Doc drove on toward Casper, Wyoming, and Yellowstone National Park. "All of Wyoming," Doc said, "should have been included in Yellowstone Park, because it's so beautiful and unspoiled." Mom agreed.

With an empty gas tank and yet another flat tire, they made camp on the beautiful banks of the North Platte River. Doc discovered that the hole in his tire was caused by a bone sliver from some animal. He carefully patched the punctured inner tube. He added gas to the tank from a small three-gallon gas can that he always carried with them.

That night they could hear and see coyotes circling all around them. These animals yelped at the moon and maybe at each other.

The next morning Mom and Doc filled the car tank and spare cans with gas in Torrington, and left for Casper. It was getting cooler now as they approached Yellowstone Park and the great Continental Divide.

Suddenly a very black and ominous-looking cloud loomed up ahead of them. It appeared to be lying almost on the ground.

"That cloud looks scary to me," Doc said. "It looks like a water spout or a tornado at sea. We must find shelter at once."

There was no shelter in sight, only desert in every direction. Doc stopped the car in the middle of the road.

"Think, Flora!" he said nervously. "What shall we do?"

Mom, calm and levelheaded, saw that her brother was too upset to make a rational decision.

"What would you do," she said to Doc, "if you were walking on a heavily wooded trail, with no gun or defense of any kind, and suddenly you looked up and saw a huge grizzly bear coming straight at you?"

"Well," said Doc, not believing his ears, "I guess you got me on that one."

"Damn it, Doc, don't wait for the answer!" yelled Mom. "Turn this Hupmobile around, and drive as fast as you can in the other direction!"

Doc spun the car around and headed back the way they had just traveled.

"You are a genius," he shouted to Mom above the roaring of the engine. "I was looking for a good excuse to see how fast this horseless carriage can move."

The Hupmobile, with an overdrive high gear in its transmission, went faster and faster. The speedometer reached fifty miles per hour, then sixty.

"Where is the fire?" shouted Mom, grinning. In all that noise and roaring wind, Doc thought she had said, "Head for the wire!" He floorboarded the gas pedal and didn't listen any more to Mom because he couldn't hear a thing over the noise of the motor anyhow.

They watched the speedometer needle reach seventy and then eighty and climb still higher. Mom saw that the storm had swerved southeast, and felt they were safe from it now. She started to worry that they were in more danger from the high speed. She watched for her chance, and when Doc wasn't looking, she turned off the ignition key, pulled it and quickly dropped it down her blouse.

Doc thought something had gone wrong with his car's big four-cylinder, four-inch-bore engine. He braked it to a dusty stop.

"Well, Flora," Doc said, trying to sound cheerful, "For me, working on a car is a lot like working on a sick or injured person. I'll diagnose the problem and have her fixed in no time."

Mom nodded solemnly. She climbed stiffly out of the Hupmobile and walked off into the beautiful flowering desert to limber up and get her circulation back to normal. Doc was carefully examining his car that had nothing wrong with it, except for a missing key.

Mom enjoyed the quiet of this now-sunny afternoon. When she returned later, refreshed and happy, she found Doc with his behind pointing at the sky, muttering to himself. He was still looking for that something, anything, that had shut down his engine. Mom thought with great care about what she should say.

"Is it ready to run, Doc?" she asked sweetly.

"Hell, no!" Doc shouted. "I've had my head under this hot engine hood ever since you've been gone." He emerged, red-faced and wiping his greasy black hands on a rag.

Mom nodded without saying anything more to him.

"Right now I have got to try to make it over to that big

rock to hide behind," said Doc, "before I can finish my work on this damn bucket of bolts."

Mom saw her chance and quickly put the ignition key back in its place. When Doc returned, he was still mad. He violently kicked the dusty tires, saying, "Where in the hell is my trusty horse?" After more unnecessary profanity, he slid behind the steering wheel. He pressed his foot on the starter pedal and turned the ignition key. To his great surprise, the powerful engine roared to life.

"Damn," said Doc, his face slowly breaking into a smile, "am I a good mechanic or what? I knew she would go when I got through making all of those tricky carburetor adjustments."

Doc was so proud of his work, Mom said nothing to him about her trickery. Whenever she told this story to us later, she said she felt that Doc really needed all the enthusiasm this little victory over the Hupmobile had given him.

He turned the car around and headed back west toward Riverton again. They barely made it before midnight. They found a place to eat and a room to sleep in for the rest of the night.

They were soon back on the road again, heading for Yellowstone Park, the Grand Teton Mountains, and Jackson Lake. They were getting higher in elevation and the temperature was getting cooler all the time as they traveled through Wind River country.

That evening they reached Dubois, Wyoming, where the air was crisp and fresh. They had another good bed and good-tasting food that night. The next morning, on the tenth day of their journey, they found almost all of the young teenagers in the town gathered around Doc's car. The youngsters were very interested in these tourists because none of them had ever seen a Hupmobile before.

"Who are you?" they asked, thinking they might be talking to celebrities.

"I am a Navy medic," Doc replied, "and this is my sister Flora. We are on a trip from Indiana to Twin Falls, Idaho, to visit our brother, Scott."

Doc looked like a boy again, Mom told us, while he was talking to these eager youngsters and as he nudged the big engine to life. He took some of the pretty teenage girls for a spin around town, and they loved it.

"How fast will she go?" asked one teenage boy.

"Yesterday," Doc said, "we were threatened by a tornado bearing down on us fast. We had to turn around quickly and outrun it." He paused modestly, then continued, "This car has a high-speed transmission and was doing over eighty as we left the storm far behind. In fact, this car may have saved our lives, and we could have gone even faster on better roads."

"With its top down," said one admiring boy, "this Hupmobile looks like it is doing eighty or more, just sitting still!" Doc really liked this observation, and thanked him for it.

Doc waved grandly, and all of the teenagers waved back and wished the visitors a safe trip.

Doc soon caught himself driving sixty miles per hour and said, "Flora, I'm sorry, I didn't realize I was driving that fast."

"I know," Mom replied. "I started watching your speedometer at fifty, but the roads here are so straight and smooth now, I didn't worry at all. And after eighty yesterday, sixty doesn't seem fast at all."

Soon they saw the beautiful cloud-piercing Teton peaks in the distance. They just had to stop and park by the roadside and admire the magnificent mountains.

"Doc," Mom whispered after awhile, "there is an Indian behind us looking at your car." Doc casually looked around.

"It's all right, Flora," he replied, "he doesn't look like he will do us any harm. I will give him a cigar or something."

The Indian spoke up and in fair English said, "Good day, sir, nice car you have."

"Yes," Doc answered, "it *is* a good car and a tough car."

The man looked around the car some more, then said, "Will you show it to my people?" He pointed down a dim road to an aspen grove.

"Sure, my friend," said Doc, giving him a cigar. "It's about time for us to make an early camp anyhow."

Doc motioned for the Indian to climb in. The Indian paused for a moment, then got in. In the grove they found a close-knit family of about twenty-five Indians camped around a beautiful spring at the head of a small creek. Five large teepees stood in a clearing. A dressed deer carcass hung from a high pole. Women, kids, two dogs, and several loose horses wandered peacefully through the aspens.

Doc willingly showed off his Hupmobile and gave rides to the whole tribe. It was almost dark when he got the job completed.

These good people insisted that Doc and Mom eat roast venison, potatoes, sourdough bread, and herb tea with them. Even years later, they remembered this Indian food as particularly delicious.

Doc broke out two pounds of pipe tobacco to give to the men. Mom found another sack of store-bought hard candy and passed it out to the women and children.

The next morning at breakfast, Doc waved at one of the big Indians just as Mom was handing Doc a plate. Doc's hand hit the bottom of the plate, and food flew all over the place. Mom and Doc stood there embarrassed, not knowing what might be coming next.

A big Indian strode up to Doc, looked at the mess, and started laughing, along with the rest of the tribe. Then the dogs raced in and wolfed down Doc's food. Doc got another big breakfast and enjoyed it thoroughly.

They said lots of good-byes as they headed out for Jackson Lake, the place where they had originally intended to camp the night before. Now they were very glad they had stopped to admire the beautiful Grand Teton Mountains. If they hadn't they would have never met these wonderful and forgotten Indian people—one of the highlights of their trip to Idaho.

That night after dark they finally did camp at Jackson Lake. The next morning, twelve days out, they enjoyed a beautiful sight—the Tetons towering right up through breathtaking white clouds and then reflecting back into the glassy lake waters.

They drove beneath the Tetons for awhile, then reached Yellowstone Park. While they were there they were held up from time to time by three black bears and two grizzly bears. They saw cars that had been damaged by the bears—doors were ripped off, windshields were smashed, and they heard that sometimes passengers were hurt or killed. In those days they were told to carry food along to throw to the bears, but not to stop for them. Now the Yellowstone Park rangers advise people never to feed any of the animals.

Uncle Doc and Mom saw sights at the park that are no longer attractions, such as Grasshopper Mountain, geysers that are now inactive, and paint pots that are long gone. Visitors to Yellowstone Park seldom see grizzly bears anymore.

Doc and Mom camped overnight at the famous Old Faithful geyser and then hurried on. They were getting more anxious every day to see their brother in Idaho.

|43|

GREAT SURPRISES IN IDAHO

Uncle Doc and Mom left Yellowstone Park early in the morning and headed south for the thriving little railroad town of Pocatello, Idaho. This was a very long drive in those days. They arrived late at night and found a hotel room to sleep in. For awhile they heard the lonesome sound of train whistles, and then they heard nothing.

After a good breakfast the next morning in one of the many cafes in Pocatello, they drove south to Lava Hot Springs, where they stayed, in spite of themselves, for two days sunning and swimming in the wonderful natural hot mineral waters, soothing aches from their long automobile trip.

After leaving Lava Hot Springs on their sixteenth day, they found that the roads west into Eden, Idaho, were surprisingly good. With an early start, they made it all the way to their long-awaited reunion at the Jones farm by early evening. Scott and Ella had no idea that Doc was on leave from the Navy or that Doc had a car, since the Hupmobile was the first car Doc owned in his life.

They drove into Scott's driveway in the big new roadster with its top down. Scott didn't even recognize them at first. He had been away from Indiana for many years working in Washington, Oregon, Montana, and now Idaho.

They found Scott and Ella in the middle of canning, and their house was a mess. Scott was speechless, and Ella was dumbfounded. For Uncle Doc and Mom, this made the long trip worthwhile. It was the surprise element that they had wanted most.

The next day Doc and Mom started to help out with the canning. In no time flat they were all having a great time. Working together, they finished quickly.

Uncle Scott was a large man weighing more than two hundred and fifty pounds, and he was all muscle. He worked hard, and he seldom drank alcohol.

"This special surprise visit calls for whiskey," he said to his brother. "Let's run into town and get us a bottle."

Doc agreed, thinking it was one of Scott's better ideas. They came back with a full quart of one hundred proof. Neither one of them was used to drinking, and though they drank just a little, they both got far too much.

Mom and Ella were not happy with them, and so for their part of the celebrating the women decided to drive to Twin Falls and go to a moving picture show.

The next morning Doc and Scott had two large hangovers, but the two women were feeling great and had gotten better acquainted.

When he felt better, Scott came up with an idea. "We may not see you two for a long time again, so why don't we all take a trip together? We can go up to the Sawtooth and Lost River mountains. They say it is wild country and Ella and I haven't seen it yet."

Mom wanted to die just thinking about more traveling sitting on her tired and sore behind. She saw that everyone else thought the idea was a great one, so she didn't say anything about how she really felt. She had seen plenty of mountains and didn't care to see more just now, even if they were the spectacular Sawtooth Mountains of Idaho.

Doc was all for the idea of seeing Idaho's scenery with Scott and Ella. He immediately started to plan for the trip.

"Since we are going into such a wild place, we should have a gun of some kind," Doc said. "I will go to Twin Falls and get a new one."

The two Jones brothers went to Twin Falls, and Doc bought a new twenty-two Browning Automatic, the first automatic gun any of them had ever seen or heard of.

They decided to take two cars, Scott's Buick and Doc's Hupmobile. By the end of the day they were all packed and ready to go at the first light of morning.

They watched the sun rise as they drove north toward the little mining town of Bellevue, Idaho, the gateway to the Great Sawtooth Mountains. This was the nineteenth day of their vacation. They made their first camp for the night in the Bellevue City Park on the banks of the Big Wood River.

Bellevue was made famous by its silver mining queen, Minnie Moore. She made millions of dollars from her mine, and that put Bellevue on the map. Bellevue was known and celebrated in England, where Minnie Moore bought all of her fine clothes and jewelry. She also bought all kinds of furnishings in England for her beautiful mansion, which still stands in excellent shape about one mile south of Bellevue.

They baked potatoes and fried fresh rainbow trout. They made and cooked cornbread in their Dutch oven and brewed coffee. It was a fine meal. They sat around the campfire "shooting the breeze" until bedtime.

They left early, and carefully made their way up the treacherous switchbacks to the steep and dreaded Galena Summit. The gorgeous scenery made it hard to watch the road.

In the Stanley Basin country, the magnificent Sawtooth peaks loomed up very close on their left. Even Mom was glad that she had decided to come along. She was falling in love with this wild Idaho country and was very happy to be with her family again.

The air was crisp, clear, and appetizing. When they reached Fourth of July Creek, they stopped and broke out some of their good Oldenburg, Indiana, beer to drink along with their homemade sandwiches.

They rolled into Stanley, a little city in the Idaho Alps. There they saw a man making a soapbox speech, and they stayed awhile to listen along with the natives. The man was a buggy salesman, and he was angrily condemning the automobile for its effect on the environment. When he pointed to their Buick and Hupmobile parked nearby, they decided it was a good time to leave town.

As they drove along they enjoyed watching the crystal-clear main Salmon River. It and four sister tributaries, among the most beautiful mountain rivers in Idaho, join one by one and enter the mighty Snake River near Riggins, Idaho.

While it was still daylight, they made camp at the little town of Sunbeam. A seventy-foot-high dam, called the Sunbeam Dam, had been built there to supply electric power to the little mining towns of Bonanza and Custer and to their two gold mines.

The electric power was carried by three copper wires on poles for about fourteen miles up Yankee Fork, the smallest of the five forks of the Salmon River system. The lines went to Bonanza then on to the two gold mines, which were about one mile apart.

They talked to some of the natives and heard a lot of their stories about the early days when big money, wild women, booze, and six-gun toters were plentiful. When you played poker you sat on the edge of your chair with one hand at your open gun holster and watched everyone at the table with your poker eye. Sometimes when a poker player reached for his rotgut whiskey, everyone else went for their guns. Then the player would quickly hold up his glass and say, "Where is the barkeep?" This would satisfy the suspicious players, and everyone would calm down again.

In those days nobody slept much at night, or at any other time, due to the bad boys. The men in those days made it a rule never to drink from a bucket, because the big rim blocked their vision and they couldn't see what the rest of the gunslingers were up to. Mom said she had never heard such wild stories, not even from Grandpaw Jones.

The next morning, the foursome left Sunbeam and motored up Yankee Fork. The water was literally alive with salmon. They were spawning, and could not go up the Salmon River any farther because they were blocked by the Sunbeam Dam at the confluence of the Salmon River and Yankee Fork.

The four stopped in Bonanza. Quite a few people still lived

there even though the mines had been shut down for a year.

They found a talkative old-timer with a group of his friends, and Scott asked him for some directions.

"Can you tell me where the famous Custer and Bonanza gold mines are?" Scott asked.

"Just follow the road on up Yankee Fork, but don't take off on Jordan Creek, just out of town a ways."

"Thank you, sir," Scott said to the old-timer. "By the way, can one hunt bear around here?"

"Well," the old fellow replied, "no, you can't, since you mention it."

"Why not, is the season closed?" Scott asked.

"No," replied the old-timer. "It's because we are decent people here, and will not tolerate anyone out there with no clothes on, and besides that, it is too damn cold anyhow!"

Everyone laughed and enjoyed the joke on Scott.

"Go ahead and hunt," the old fellow said, wiping tears of laughter from his eyes. "You can do damn-near anything else you want to here, too. There are bear here, but you would be awful lucky if you saw one."

THE DAY THE MOUNTAINTOP BLEW OFF

Doc, Mom, Scott, and Ella made camp that day at Custer. This little mining town had been totally vacated when the mines closed a year earlier.

Doc and Scott looked around and noticed that Yankee Fork continued to be full of salmon by the thousands. Even the tiny tributaries had salmon in them, along with trout, but the trout were so full of eggs left by the spawning salmon that they wouldn't bite on any of Scott's bait.

Finally Doc went fishing with his bare hands, and caught a nice-looking salmon. That evening they enjoyed a fine supper of fried fresh salmon steaks with all the trimmings.

The next morning they spent hours looking around the deserted town. They wandered into a saloon, and Doc pointed out what he thought were large-caliber bullet holes in the saloon's floor.

"Why, that's awful," Mom said. "It looks like some poor devil was shot again even after he fell to the floor." The others agreed that she was probably right.

They all walked up Yankee Fork, leaving the town of Custer deserted again. About four miles upstream, they stumbled onto some black bears feeding on the salmon. When the bears saw people, they disappeared up the mountainside and into the forest. The four were glad the bears had not been aggressive and that they had no small cubs with them, or there could have been trouble.

About that time they decided to go back to their cars. On the way back, Doc explored an aspen grove and found a lot of honeycomb mushrooms. They were nice and fresh, and just the thing for supper. They decided it would be mushrooms, salmon steak, and cornbread that evening under the stars.

It was a long hike back to camp to prepare their food, and they had a big appetite just thinking about what good things they would eat. It didn't take long to get supper ready with everybody helping out. They had just finished eating and were sitting around the campfire talking about their blisters and tired bones, when someone asked Scott a question. He didn't answer, and was slumped over, leaning on a log.

"Is Scott all right?" Mom asked anxiously. Doc took a close look at him and felt his pulse.

"He's sound asleep," Doc said, smiling. They all followed Scott's example and soon were fast asleep.

During breakfast the next morning, they discussed what they should do that day. They decided to climb to the top of a mountain. Doc took along his new twenty-two automatic with long-rifle ammunition.

They wove back and forth through the forest, climbing higher and higher. They saw grouse, snowshoe rabbits, lots of pine squirrels, and chipmunks. After they finished eating lunch and rested for awhile, they found a beat-up old rattlesnake nearby. He didn't look good; in fact, he looked so sick that they all felt sorry for him, so they left him alone and alive.

"Maybe he couldn't stand the high elevation," Doc said, "or maybe he got the cramps from eating some of our leftover chow."

They didn't make it to the top of the mountain because they decided they had done enough climbing to last for a day or two. Before they started back down toward Custer, they stopped to rest and enjoy the panoramic view.

"What is all that shiny stuff across the canyon, on that other mountainside?" Mom asked Ella.

"It looks like it may be a junkyard," Ella answered.

Doc used his twenty-four power binoculars to carefully study the site.

"It looks like it is mostly tin cans of various sizes, glass bottles, and a lot of round five-gallon cans," Doc said.

They were about six hundred feet straight across the canyon from the mountain junkyard. They sat down in the shade under a large pine tree while they looked at it. They talked about how shameful it was to leave so much junk in that beautiful country, and how the Indians would never have created such an eyesore.

"Flora and Ella," Doc said, picking up his new twenty-two rifle, "pick out a can for me to shoot at. I'll rip it to pieces with my new Browning. This will be my first shot with my new rifle."

"Shoot at that big one under the pine tree, there on top of the pile," Mom said.

"Good," replied Doc. "That one is easy to see without binoculars."

He took good steady aim and let go with one round. Well, they didn't even hear his twenty-two fire, because of a monstrous explosion. A spectacular fireball rose two hundred feet in the air over the junkyard. Across the canyon from them the whole mountaintop seemed to have blown up. An astonishing dust cloud climbed high into the sky. Deep echoes rumbled up and down the canyon for several seconds, and pine needles showered down on them from the big pine tree they were sitting under. Little dust devils were raised all over the mountainside they were on when the concussion hit. They felt the hot blast, and those who were standing were almost knocked to the ground.

They were lucky—no one was hurt. A dark mushroom cloud rose high in the sky above them, and looked like it would hang in the quiet air for a long time.

"*Holy horse biscuits!*" Scott croaked, looking at Doc's gun. "What kind of a gun did you buy? You blew up the whole damn mountainside, and probably changed the scenery for years to come!"

Doc just stood there looking at the gun in his hands. He couldn't believe it.

They were afraid that someone would come after them and throw them all in jail. Doc unloaded his gun completely, and they scrambled down the mountainside to their cars as fast as they could. They quickly gathered up their camping gear and bedrolls and drove away. Looking for seclusion, they drove up a bad road into the canyon as far as they could go, then turned the cars around to have a quick getaway if necessary.

They camped in this out-of-the-way place until about two o'clock in the morning, then left. They passed through Bonanza as quietly as possible, on down Yankee Fork to Sunbeam, and then on to Challis, without stopping.

They made camp on the main Salmon River, out of sight, and stayed there all that day and night. They still didn't know for sure what had caused the enormous explosion.

Scott had worked for a few years in the copper pits and mines at Anaconda, Montana, and he knew a little about mining. He started to think about possible causes.

"That junkyard of cans and other containers," Scott said, "must have had some nitroglycerin in it. It's sometimes used, along with dynamite, for blasting tunnels for gold and other types of mining. It is highly explosive on impact or exposure to sudden heat." After hearing more about nitroglycerin, the others decided that Scott was probably right.

|45|

CRATERS OF THE MOON

Feeling lucky to be alive and not in jail, the four decided to "visit the moon." They traveled over Willow Creek Pass and down the Big Lost River, passing some of the highest mountains in Idaho. Years later, one of these mountains, 12,662 feet in elevation, was named to honor Idaho's famous senator, William Edgar Borah.

That evening, they camped at Twin Springs. These springs run a constant river of cold water down the east side of Twin Springs Pass and into Little Lost River. The river flows several miles down a beautiful wide valley, passing the town of Arco and flowing on into the Big Butte desert. There the river disappears into the porous lava and is lost underground into the aquifer, thus the name Lost River.

The next day they arrived at a place unlike any other on Earth—the Craters of the Moon, created by volcanic activity about two thousand years ago.

On the road again, they reentered Bellevue, completing a giant and eventful circle. They spent the night in the Bellevue City Park in a thunder and lightning storm, and made it back to the farm in Eden late in next evening, "tired, dizzy with happiness, and addicted to the road," Mom wrote in her diary.

After twenty-seven days of driving, the Hupmobile needed some attention. Following breakfast the next morning, Uncle Doc immediately started to service it for the long trip back to Indiana.

"Doc," Mom said, "I want to rest and visit with Scott and Ella for a few more days. If you like, you can stay longer, or head back by yourself. You know I love to ride on the train, and I can go back that way."

Doc thought about this for awhile and did some calculating about how many days he needed to make the trip.

"Flora," Doc said, "I will need to head out with the Hupmobile early tomorrow morning in order to be back in New York before my Navy leave is up. You take the train, and you can rest through the two thousand miles back home to Indiana."

But by now Mom had started to think of Idaho as home.

|46|

A TRICK ON DOC IN INDIANA

When Uncle Doc arrived at our place in Indiana after about only eleven days on the road, he got a big welcome from all of us, including Mom, who had arrived earlier on the train. Even Lummox and Just Plain Cat showed Doc that they were happy to see him.

Doc was in good shape, but tired and hungry. Mrs. Milbourne cooked him a large supper, and then he went back to the hay wagon to sleep.

The next morning, Uncle Doc decided to give his Hupmobile a good inspection job. He wanted to make any repairs that were needed before going to New York Harbor to board his hospital ship. Doc thought of himself as an extra good mechanic after fixing the Hupmobile in Wyoming, when actually Mom had just hidden the key for awhile and then replaced it.

Doc was convinced that a four-thousand-mile round trip, plus a rough side trip of about four hundred miles into the Sawtooth and Lost River mountains, would call for some adjustments to the engine and to the drive train.

On the spur of the moment, I invented a trick that I wanted to pull on Uncle Doc. Then I thought to myself, "No, this trick is way too mean to pull on Uncle Doc." But I couldn't get it off my mind, as it was tickling me too much. Then I thought, "Oh well, what the heck are tricks for anyway—I'll do it!"

I quickly found two round rocks, each about the size of a goose egg. I stood in front of the Hupmobile by the radiator out of Doc's way. Uncle Doc started the big engine and idled it to check for any unusual sounds. I started clicking my two rocks together, keeping perfect time with the engine. He would listen, then rev it up. I clicked faster when he revved it up, still keeping perfect time.

"*Damn it!*" he shouted. "I just can't believe it."

With an amazed look on his face, Uncle Doc hollered for Uncle Harry. Uncle Harry had worked in garages for years and was a pretty good mechanic.

They both listened, first as the engine was idling, and then as it was revved up.

"You got a rod, or maybe a main bearing, going out," said Uncle Harry. "It sounds to me more like a rod."

"I was lucky to make it back home with this car before that damn bearing went out and flattened my crank shaft," Doc moaned.

Uncle Harry got all of his mechanic's tools out. While I sat on the running board out of sight, Doc carefully drove his car over the pit that was made for working on cars. With the engine idling, they could listen to it more carefully from underneath and make sure of what they had heard. I sat behind them with my two rocks clicking in perfect time with the engine.

Suddenly they both turned around and saw that it was me doing the clicking and not the engine! I was stunned by their sudden movement. They both tried to grab me, and I ran like a goose at feather-pluckin' time. But before I got a good start and really turned on my champion speed, they caught me. They both wanted to spank me, but when one started the other yelled and stopped him. Neither would let the other do it. This, along with the relief they felt that the Hupmobile was okay, led them to start laughing.

Mom heard the big commotion and came out to see what was going on. My two uncles told her what I had done to them. Mom immediately gave me a real paddling, and nobody tried to stop her.

"Someday," Uncle Harry said, "this tricky little kid will hit on to something worthwhile—if somebody don't kill him first for playing tricks on them."

I knew my Dad thought it was a clever idea, since I heard him telling some of our neighbors about it. Dad said I had made an engine-knocking sound with rocks that had fooled his two brothers-in-law, and they were both good mechanics.

Uncle Doc left his fully serviced Hupmobile at our place and caught a train. He made it back to New York on time to board his hospital ship before his leave ran out, which was amazing considering all he had been through in a short period of time.

|47|

HENRY KARNS' NEW STARTER

While Mom and Uncle Doc were on their trip to Idaho, a family by the name of Karns moved into a small farmhouse nearby and became our new neighbors.

Henry, the oldest of the Karns boys, was twenty. He was very ambitious and was always making money one way or another. Our family liked him and could see he was becoming interested in Dollie.

One October evening, Henry came by to ask Mom and Dad if he could take Dollie to a Halloween party on the following evening. He told them that he had saved his money and bought his first new automobile. Mom and Dad asked Henry some questions, and finally Dad said, "Yes, Dollie may go to the party with you, if she wants to go."

Henry asked her, and she answered with a shy "Yes, I'll go."

The next evening Henry was there early. He wanted to show us his beautiful black automobile before he took Dollie to the party.

"This automobile," he told us, "is called a Saxon and is the very latest and most modern car available. It has a new type of starter that doesn't use a crank." Henry's new starter became the center of attention for the men.

Henry showed us how a three-fourths-inch rope was attached to a wheel at the front end of the crank pin. The rope ran from the grooved wheel up through the dashboard, where it was tied in a large knot.

The engine was started by grasping hold of the knot and giving it a quick, hard pull to turn the engine one revolution. This action was repeated until the engine started. It worked very much like our small rope-starting engines of today.

We were all amazed by the inventiveness of the brilliant engineers of such convenient modern devices.

We also watched Dollie with Henry. We could tell that while she had not forgotten about the tragedy of her first love, George Shebler, she had begun to put it behind her.

Henry Karns was closer to her age and was very handsome and ambitious. He was getting a solid financial start by buying an eighty-acre farm on a shoestring. Henry's plan was to purchase a small sawmill and use it to pay for his farm. Later he sawed hundreds of large trees into railroad ties and sold them to railroad companies, making big money, and at the same time clearing his land for future crops.

After showing us his new car up close, Henry drove it around to the roadside and parked it behind the trees and shrubbery in front of our house. Everyone walked back to the house except me. It was Halloween, and I wanted to play a trick.

I got the car jack out of our Maxwell and quietly jacked up one of the rear wheels on Henry's Saxon. When the wheel was about one inch off the ground, I placed an old block of wood under the rear axle. Then I removed the jack and returned it to our Maxwell.

I hurried back into the house, being very careful to not be seen. I went upstairs and stationed myself at a bedroom window where I could watch the fun through the tree limbs.

It was starting to get dark when Henry and Dollie came out of the house with Mom and Dad. The young couple happily waved good-bye and went on out to the new Saxon. Henry gallantly opened the car door and helped Dollie in.

The engine started beautifully on the first try. I could hear the gears click as Henry engaged them. He gave the Saxon some gas and I thought I saw him lean forward as if he was trying to help the car get going, but nothing moved. The shiny new Saxon just sat there.

At this point I felt sorry for them. I truly felt that I had overdone it. I would have run down right then and confessed—but I knew that my sister would kill me on the spot if I did.

I heard Henry rev up the motor several times. Then he got out and walked around the car. I saw him peering over the shrubbery to see if Mom and Dad were still standing there, but they had gone back into the house.

I imagined he was probably telling Dollie that this had never happened before, and that the car would probably go after it had warmed up a bit. Dollie got out of the car, said something to Henry, and went to the house.

Soon Oscar and Dad walked out to give Henry some advice, but none of their instructions worked. Henry climbed behind the steering wheel and revved it up, while Dad violently shook the Saxon. I hoped and expected that the Saxon would drop off my wood block and get going down the road, and then my Dad would be declared a "mechanical hero." However, this did not happen.

When I saw Lester heading downstairs, I went down with him, and we joined Henry and the other men outside.

Everyone was relieved when my Uncle Harry showed up. He was a good mechanic. First, he listened to the Saxon's motor while it idled, scratched his head, and spit some tobacco. Next, he crawled under the car and felt the temperature of the drive train and the differential. He listened carefully for any unusual sounds. Nothing. Then his eyes must have gotten used to the dark, because he spotted the old wooden block, still propped firmly under the axle of the left rear wheel.

Uncle Harry scrambled out from under the car uttering a stream of profanity. In between the swear words I heard him shout, "*Where in the devil is that Harold?*"

I turned around in the darkness and blindly ran square into Henry Karns, knocking myself to the ground. I got up and sneaked quietly off into the night.

"Henry, you and Dollie have been had by Harold," I heard Uncle Harry say. "He's played a Halloween trick on you both."

Uncle Harry dusted off his clothes and continued, "There is no doubt in my mind who done it. He got Doc and me just a few weeks ago. He had us believing that a rod was going out on Doc's Hupmobile, and he did it just by clicking two rocks together."

When Dollie got the news, she came out on the porch and I heard her say, "I am going to skin that kid alive—it will be more painful for him than just killing him."

I knew she meant it. For a long time I had to leave a cold trail and stay a mile ahead of her at all times.

Ol' Henry, however, said he thought it was a good trick. He listened to my apologies several times and also played the part of peacemaker. Dollie was still after my scalp, but I was finally able to shout my apologies to her with only about a half-mile between us.

"It takes lots of creativeness," Henry told me, "to come up with tricks that are original like that one." Henry Karns was a good fellow in my eyes, and I enjoyed his willingness to laugh about such things.

|48|

THE INDIANA STATE FAIR

Some weeks later, we were all sitting at the dinner table, worn out and not saying much.

"We have all been working hard from early until late, doing the many jobs and chores that it takes to run a farm operation like this one," Dad said, "and a vacation is past due." We all agreed.

"I want a vote," Dad continued, "on either going to the State Fair in Indianapolis, or on staying home and going back to work." The vote was unanimous in favor of the State Fair.

We loaded our camping equipment into two big boxes that fit on the long running boards of the Maxwell. This was the way most people traveled then because there were no motels and very few hotels. We planned to stay for two or three days. When we arrived in Indianapolis, Dad and Oscar set up the tents in a large tree-covered park.

Me and Lester had never been to Indianapolis before, and we were having the time of our lives. The first thing we did was get lost. We missed our supper, and worried Mom and Dad sick.

Near dark, a policeman saw us crying and came over to see what our troubles were. We told him that we couldn't find our Mom and Dad.

"Not to worry," he laughed. "I'll help you find your parents."

He took each of us by the hand and began walking.

"When I was a small boy, I got myself lost, too," he told us, "and a policeman helped me find my Mom and Dad." It wasn't long before we spotted our Maxwell and our tents. We left the policeman in a cloud of dust and ran into the waiting arms of Mom and Dad. The policeman came up to the folks to reassure them. They thanked him for finding us.

"Don't worry, this happens all the time at our State Fair," he said.

Brave now, I asked my policeman friend, "What is that club hanging from your belt?"

"That is called a night stick," he replied.

"Do you sometimes carry a day stick, too?"

With a big grin he explained, "It's very simple—when the sun comes up each morning, my night stick turns into a day stick." I figured that was a very clever answer, and I looked at him with even more respect.

After the policeman left, we received a paddling from our parents for getting lost, and we were not allowed out of their sight again, unless Oscar was with us.

Oscar thought it was terrible to whip us so he went off with us and bought us our first Coca-Cola. We had never tasted it before, in fact, we had never even heard of it. I didn't like it much; it tasted like soap suds to me, and we were well-acquainted with soap suds because Mom washed our mouths out with them whenever we said something nasty.

Dad came back to our tents with a sixty-pound watermelon. He told us he had stolen it, and we were worried to think that Dad would steal a big watermelon from some Indianapolis melon patch. We were relieved to learn that he had really just bought the first-prize-winning melon of the fair.

Then me and Lester saw our first moving picture show. I didn't like the picture show because it jiggled a lot. Words would appear, but I couldn't read fast enough, particularly some of the bigger words. When the man on the screen kissed the pretty lady, he didn't do it like Dad kissed Mom. This guy would bend the lady clear over backwards.

"That show was a waste of money," I told Mom and Dad afterwards. "I don't think that picture shows will make it, unless everybody in the country learns to read real fast. But the music wasn't too bad."

The show that we *really* loved was the speed cyclist. This man wore really tight, brightly colored clothing, and he rode his bicycle down a steep platform doing loop-the-loops at the blistering speed of sixty miles per hour. He had two large signs, one on each side of his ramp, reading, "World's Fastest Cyclist, A Mile A Minute or Sixty Miles Per Hour!"

The loop was seventy feet across, and we were amazed at the size of it. Me and Lester got as close as we could to the ramp without getting on it. We didn't want to miss a thing he did while performing his loop-the-loops. He was great, and after his performance was over he walked right up to us, leaned over and said, "Boys, don't try to do this one on your roller skates." We just couldn't believe that the fastest cyclist in the whole world had talked to us! We talked about it for days.

|49|

FIRE ON THE ROAD

We left for home on the third day. Oscar was driving the Maxwell and we were about ten miles from home when it started getting dark.

"I can hear a new rattle in the engine compartment," Oscar said. "It may be wise to stop and see what it is before damage is done."

He pulled off to the side of the road as far as possible and parked. It was hard for us to see under the hood, and we needed some light. The lanterns were packed away in one of the long boxes strapped on the Maxwell's running boards. Rather than going to all the trouble of getting out a lantern, Oscar decided to use a match.

With the engine shut off, Oscar held his match out, looked very closely under the hood, and saw nothing wrong. Then he crawled under the car. By matchlight he spotted a small bolt lying up in the oil pan.

"I can't see any place where that bolt came from," he said. "Maybe it was lost there during the manufacturing of the Maxwell. I need another match to see good enough to retrieve the bolt from the oil pan. Maybe later I can find the place where it is missing from."

Oscar didn't notice that the carburetor was leaking raw gasoline. This time Oscar's match ignited the leaking gas. A whooshing explosion followed—with Oscar still under the car and in the middle of the blaze!

Mom and Dad, standing in the flames themselves, grabbed Oscar's feet and quickly pulled him out of the fire. Oscar was lucky that he did not have any gasoline or grease on his clothes, or he might have caught fire.

Scared, we kept moving back into the woods. We were forced back more than a hundred feet away from the fire. We were trying to make sure we were all safe, and gather our wits, when the Maxwell's gas tank exploded, creating a frightening fireball that illuminated the semi-darkness of the countryside as brightly as day. Our faithful old Maxwell and all of our camping gear was consumed by the raging fire.

Soon two other cars stopped to help. One of them was our neighbor, Mr. Cord Shekel. After the fire burned down, and nothing was left but the metal frame of our Maxwell, Mr. Shekel loaded us into his large black Hudson and drove us home.

We lost everything in the fire except the clothes we were

wearing and our lives. Oscar had some serious burns on his face, hands, and arms, but he was strong and healed quickly.

|50|

A DOUBLE-UNANIMOUS VOTE

After Oscar recovered from his burns, he called us all together, including Arlie Rust and Mrs. Milbourne.

"Listen to me very closely," Oscar said, "because this is a big and costly decision for all of us. I am calling for a vote, and even you, Arlie, and you, Mrs. Milbourne, could be affected by the outcome."

We sat quietly while Oscar explained his proposal.

"Now, all in favor of Dad and me buying a brand new Maxwell, hold up your hands."

Eighteen hands were counted and there were only nine people present. A double-unanimous decision had been reached. Oscar phoned in an order for a new black Maxwell to the Joe Cashbaum Garage, and the car was delivered that same day from Brookville.

Me and Lester were kept busy for hours just looking at it, not letting each other touch it for fear of leaving a finger print or a jelly smear from one of the half-eaten sandwiches that we were always too busy to finish.

The new Maxwell looked so different from our old one. Its streamlined engine hood was much lower, and its body was much longer. The speedometer read an incredible fifty-miles-per-hour top speed. It even had an electric horn button on the left side of the dashboard. The old Maxwell's horn had been a large rubber ball that you had to squeeze. The new Maxwell also had smaller wheels and larger rubber tires. This made the car much lower to the road and gave it a softer ride. The new gas tank was at the rear end, instead of under the front seat.

Dad smiled and said he didn't have to worry about sitting in the front seat any more.

"Why is that, Dad?" I asked, puzzled.

"It's just that was worried about starving to death," he said. "You see, if the gas tank blew up, it would be days before I would get back to the ground—unless I could grab a chicken hawk snack up there somewhere."

Whenever we went to town in our new car, we passed our old burned-out Maxwell. The blackened, rusting frame sat at the side of the road for almost two years. For a long time I had bad dreams about the awful fire eating up our beautiful old Maxwell.

It took Lummox a long time to get used to our new Maxwell. He kept his distance and barked at it every time it moved. He kept inching closer to it all the time, though, until one day that crazy dog must have spent thirty minutes just wetting down the wheels. We knew he was ready to claim the car as his own when we saw him standing at the back end one day, carefully looking at the spare wheel and tire. I think ol' Lummox was wondering how he was going to get that one watered down, too.

Just Plain Cat must have liked the new Maxwell, too. We always had to remove him from the front seat whenever we wanted to go somewhere.

"The new Maxwell should have a garage," Mom and Dad said. "It should be out of the hot sun and weather."

A vote was taken on whether or not to build a double garage. The vote was again in favor. We justified the expense because it would make the farm worth more, and we all considered it to be a good investment.

Herman Walters, a neighbor of ours, was hired to be the construction foreman. Herman was a carpenter by trade and a wonderful yodeler. Herman could yodel so loud that he could be heard nearly a mile away. Everybody knew when he was on the job, because he yodeled only when he was working.

It wasn't long before a lot of neighbors heard about the new garage and came around wanting to help. We had at least forty people who were ready to work. With everyone helping, the big garage was finished in only two and a half days. The new Maxwell had its own house, with a complete workshop, built-in work pit, and an overhead traveling chain fall.

As a result, the new Maxwell remained looking good longer than it would have if it had been parked out in the weather. Automobile paint wasn't as good then as it is now, and cars would tarnish and fade quickly if they were not protected.

Uncle Doc's well-traveled Hupmobile shared the other half of the new garage with our second Maxwell for many years.

|51|

BENDER'S NEW SHOTGUN

Walter Cummins, Dad's tenant tobacco grower, was a good man and a hard worker. He had a son named Clarence, a big kid about four years older than me who me and Lester called "Bender."

Mr. Cummins often took Bender out in the woods and fields to hunt rabbits, squirrels, or anything else that could grace their dinner table. Mr. Cummins took special care to train Bender in how to safely carry and fire a shotgun, and how to hit what he aimed at.

Mr. Cummins would let me go along with them sometimes. It was always my job to carry whatever they were killing, and I didn't like the job much. However, they told me there was nothing wrong with killing animals if they were used for food. Mr. Cummins said that he needed this extra food for his large family, and at my tender young age, I was easily convinced.

The hunting went on mostly during the fall and winter months, and Bender became a fine marksman, so Mr. Cummins bought a new twelve-gauge shotgun for him, even though he could not afford to. Mr. Cummins was very proud of Bender, and would have gone even further out on a limb to please his favorite son.

During several hunting trips with them, I could see that Bender's care and mindfulness of his new shotgun was fading. Bender and his gun were becoming one big dangerous weapon.

I felt safe, though, because I always followed along behind him. His dog was in the lead to scare up game for him to blast away at. Ol' Bender seemed to never miss.

On a hunt with Bender one day, his dog found a rabbit and started to chase it. We began to run to keep up. I was a fast runner and stayed right behind Bender. Suddenly Bender stopped and lifted his shotgun to fire at the rabbit.

I was watching the rabbit, too, and I smashed right into Bender and knocked him off balance. The shotgun was knocked from its firing position, and it blasted away when Bender stumbled.

Bender and his dog were very close to the rabbit, and when the shotgun went off, all three of them fell to the ground. The poor dog got the wadding and three or four pellets from the shell in his rear end and the rabbit got the remainder of the shot.

My own blood was streaming from my nose where I had collided with the butt of his gun. It hurt something awful, and I started crying. The dog howled and ran off into the woods wailing. Bender slowly picked his oversize body up off the ground.

"Who shot my dog?" he demanded.

"You did!" I replied.

We wound up at my house first. Mom was putting some big loaves of homemade bread on an outdoor cooling rack in our backyard.

She looked up and saw us coming through the back gate with Bender leading and half-carrying me. I was covered with blood and Bender had his shotgun under his arm. Mom yelled for Oscar and Dad.

"Start up the Maxwell quick!" she shouted. "Harold has been shot in the face and shoulders."

I must have looked awful. My nosebleed had saturated the upper portion of my chest. Mom was violent with anger. She grabbed poor Bender and, with the strength of a grizzly bear, threw him through the open door of the nearby summer kitchen, then locked the door shut.

She rushed me toward the roaring Maxwell. I was trying very hard to explain to her that it was only a real bad nosebleed, that I had not been shot, and that Bender was innocent of any wrongdoing.

It was evident Mom didn't hear a word I was saying. She pushed me into the Maxwell with Dad and Oscar, and we were racing to see Dr. Cupp in Metamora before she began to examine me more closely.

"Stop the car, son!" she said to Oscar, who was driving. "Thank God, it's only a bad nosebleed."

Oscar turned the Maxwell around, and now Mom started to worry about what she had done to poor innocent Bender.

"Dear God, what have I done to that boy?" she moaned over and over again on the way home.

All I could think about was how much my Mom must love me. She was a nurse, but she had fallen completely apart when she thought I was in a life-threatening crisis.

Although my nose hurt a lot from bumping into Bender's gun, I couldn't help but feel sorry for Mom, Dad, and Oscar. This little incident had gotten out of hand, and now Bender was the one who was hurt the most.

When we arrived home, Mom ran to the summer kitchen and let Bender out. "Bender, what have I done to you?" she said. "I am so very sorry. Please forgive me!"

Mom was busy for days trying to explain her actions to Walter Cummins and his wife, but most of all to poor Bender. She even explained the whole thing a couple of times to our family. And all Bender had wanted was a rabbit for supper.

Although no one needed to feel guilty or even at fault in this accident, neither the Cummins family or the Hannebaum family did any hunting with a gun for a long time.

|52|

BENDER AND GRACIE

Bender left his shiny new shotgun in the corner of his room for a long time. He cleaned it some, and handled it often, and before long his resistance to hunting began to break down. Bender went out alone on several hunting trips, and his accuracy with his new shotgun quickly came back to him.

One morning he told his Dad and Mom that he wanted to stay out of school and shoot some rabbits for supper that evening.

"No, Clarence," his mother said, using his real name as she always did. "You must go to school and get a good education."

"We will be butchering our hog in a week or so," his Dad added, "and then we will have lots of meat for our supper table."

Bender reluctantly walked with his little brother and his sister Grace down the lane that followed Gates Branch, a little creek that joined with Pipe Creek near the main road, to where the school wagon was waiting. Gracie was about my age—nearly eight years old. She was very pretty, quiet, and well liked at school.

Like most of our days in the classroom, nothing out of the ordinary happened that day, but when it was time to get on the school wagon in the evening to go home, Ol' Bender was not there.

When we got to Gates Branch, Gracie got off the wagon with her little brother, and they walked up the lane to their house. She saw Bender coming down off the hill ahead of them. He had been rabbit hunting with his twelve-gauge shotgun, and was carrying some rabbits.

Bender waited for his little sister and brother at the Cummins' door at one end of a fifty-foot-long stone walkway to show them his rabbits and to unload the two live rounds from his shotgun. Gracie was just stepping onto the other end of the stone walkway when Bender's twelve-gauge double-barreled shotgun accidentally fired one barrel.

The barrel was pointed low toward the stone walkway and in a direct line with Gracie. The load of shot first struck the walkway close to Bender, then ricocheted up at an angle, striking Gracie full in her chest and face.

While Bender screamed for his Mom and Dad, Gracie lost consciousness. Mr. Cummins grabbed her up in his arms and took her into the house. He and his wife worked desperately to slow the bleeding.

At his father's instruction, Bender mounted a saddle horse that was standing at the hitch rack and rode at full speed the half-mile down the dirt road to our house. We had just gotten off the school wagon ourselves. We could only stand there while Bender jumped from his still-running horse and flashed past us through our front gate.

"Mr. and Mrs. Hannebaum," we heard him shouting inside. "Please come quick with your Maxwell! Gracie has been shot." Then he added with a wail, "I think she is dying!"

My folks didn't ask him even one question. Oscar drove the Maxwell with Mom and Dad in the back and Bender in the front seat.

My folks told us that when they reached the Cummins place they left the lights on and the motor running. By the car's lights they could see blood on the stone walkway.

As they ran toward the house, they were met by Mr. Cummins carrying Gracie. Oscar accelerated the car over the hills to Metamora, blowing the new electric horn to warn all traffic to get out of the way.

Dr. Cupp lived behind his office. He heard the Maxwell, with its motor roaring and its horn blowing loud and steady, and knew that an emergency was on the way. He met the car at the sidewalk in front.

Dr. Cupp quickly carried Gracie to his well-equipped emergency room, and he and his nurse worked over her with great calmness. At intervals one of them would break free to try to calm everyone else down.

Mr. Cummins told Dr. Cupp how the shot load had struck the rough stone walkway and then glanced up and struck his daughter.

"That is good news, in a way," Dr. Cupp told them. "The shot probably didn't have enough force to enter her chest cavity. The stone should have slowed the velocity of the pellets."

The shot that struck Gracie's head and face broke her skin but did not penetrate her bone structure, and the pellets that hit her in the chest area were slowed by her clothing.

"If the shotgun blast had come directly from the barrel,

Gracie would have died instantly," Dr. Cupp said.

Mr. and Mrs. Cummins looked at each other and realized that, as impossible as it might seem, this accident could have been much worse.

"I want to keep Grace overnight," said Dr. Cupp. "Be here at ten o'clock in the morning," he added, "and Mrs. Hannebaum, I want you here with Mr. and Mrs. Cummins, also. Tonight I will give Gracie a sedative so she can rest, and I will remove all the shot pellets I can find. Just don't worry, she will be fine."

That evening, Mom and Dad stayed with the Cummins family and did their best to encourage them.

The next morning, Oscar drove Mom and the whole Cummins family to Dr. Cupp's office. Dr. Cupp came in to talk to Mr. and Mrs. Cummins.

"Gracie has lost one eye, and some damage was done to her other eye," Dr. Cupp began, "but at her young age, I think the partially damaged eye will recover. I have removed all of the pellets, except one in her bad eye. Removal there is too dangerous. This one pellet will heal into the scar tissue and will never bother her, and this eye cannot recover. Maybe someday . . . " Here he stopped, not wanting to give them false hope.

Gracie healed up, but she always kept her bad eye covered with a black patch held on by an elastic band. It was tragic how her pretty face was disfigured by scars left by the pellets and by the doctor's scalpel incisions.

Gracie's friends at school didn't want to be seen with her anymore, so she played all by herself. When Mom heard about this, she held our heads against a wall in the kitchen.

"Don't ever let me or your Daddy hear of you two kids shunning or saying any bad things about Gracie," she said sharply, "either here or at school. You may as well learn to be gentlemen. Help her on and off the school wagon, walk with her to her classroom seat, and play with her outside, unless she rejects it, do you understand?"

We both nodded.

"Maybe the other kids at school will see you two helping her, and they will be kinder," she added. "We don't know what she is going through. Some people feel that when a girl loses the beauty of her face she has lost one of her most prized and precious possessions."

Mom sat down on a kitchen chair and wiped the tears from her eyes. "She must now go through her life with twice the danger of becoming totally blind, because she has only one eye, half her normal sight."

Lester and me did our best to play with Gracie and to be kind to her.

Bender took it very hard; he loved his sister very much. He told his Dad that he was no longer interested in his shotgun or in hunting. He suggested that they sell the gun and use the money to help Gracie.

From that time on, Bender was always helping and doing special things for Gracie. He was the best brother that a sister could have wished for, and he never did forget what he had done. Bender treated his sister with great love and respect, and set a good example for the rest of us.

|53|

SUMMER VACATION

School was out for the summer vacation, and this made me very happy. After breakfast I decided to just walk along Pipe Creek and look into the clear deep water, where I hoped to see a lot of big fish.

The woods were alive this morning with Mother Nature's activities. Hundreds of birds of different varieties and colors were singing and quarreling with each other. I tried hard to sing or whistle along with some of them. It was embarrassing to hear how much better the birds were than I was.

Lester and Bert said they enjoyed school, but I couldn't seem to develop any liking for it. But that question was behind me today, as I was now free, and no longer a prisoner of the school. I could be with my animal friends in the woods, and could play with some of the neighborhood kids if I wanted to.

One good thing about school was Omar Clark, my best friend. I also liked our young lady school teacher even when she penalized us for being late from lunch hour. I knew she had to do it.

I was wearing my slouchy cap, moving slowly along the creek and looking into the water, when a terrible hissing scared me. I spotted a big spreading viper not more than a yard from my bare feet, with its head raised high and its beady eyes looking at me.

Without hesitation I jumped smack into Pipe Creek, a fall of about six feet. A flock of ducks flew right out from under me, and my splash was so loud that all of the little birds around there quit singing for a little while.

I scrambled out of the water and up the steep bank to the pathway. Sure enough Mr. Snake was still waiting for me, poison fangs and all. He seemed to be pleased about all the trouble he had caused me, and slithered around like he wanted to pick a fight with me.

I wasn't about to oblige this slick operator. The thought of killing him passed through my mind, but I remembered what Dad had told us: "Nobody in this family kills anything in the woods, unless it's a life-threatening situation or for the supper table." That snake was still a ways from that on both counts.

As I walked on down the path toward the Whitewater River, I spotted a dim trail to my left. It led up a gravelly hill where a very old and nearly forgotten graveyard was hidden, almost completely covered by a tanglement of old grapevines, trees, tall bunch grass, and rotten logs and bushes.

I climbed up the hill, wanting to explore the graveyard some more. I had been there before with Mom when she was putting flowers on the graves. One of the stones was for her great-granddad, Isaac Jones. There were several others, but I couldn't understand what relations they were to us.

I looked carefully at the dates on some of the oldest headstones, some from the 1700s. I thought about these people, all related to me in one way or another, if you went back far enough. Now their monuments were almost forgotten and abandoned, and without them, I wouldn't be here today.

Then I took a look at my imaginary railroad watch and said, "Gosh, I have got to get moving on!"

Leaving the graveyard, my feet took me back to Pipe Creek and on down toward the Whitewater River. Along the way I saw a twenty-pound snapping turtle slowly working his way up a steep fifteen-foot bank, only to lose his footing at the top and tumble back into the creek.

For about a half hour I watched the poor oversized turtle try to make it up to the top of the bank. Each time he failed earlier because of his exhaustion. Finally he fell upside down near the water, lying as still as death.

I took off all my clothes, since they were now dry again, and slowly got into the water. Quietly I swam over to the turtle. He looked much larger now because I was so close to him. I carefully took hold of his big, rough, prehistoric-looking tail. I swam on my back, towing the turtle across the deep water to a little sand bar on the other side of the creek. I turned Mr. Turtle right-side up and released him on his feet.

I swam back to the other side and quickly put my clothes on, because I was cold and they felt so nice and warm from lying in the sunshine. I could see my big friend sunning and wiggling his toes happily on the small sandy beach where I had left him.

I had spent a lot of time there, so now I ran fast down the trail to make up for it. Suddenly a little animal appeared in the path, so I jumped high to keep from stepping on it. I stopped and went back to examine it. It was a fat hop toad. I remembered what Mom had told me about hop toads: "Don't touch them, or you will get warts all over you." I still gave it a good looking at, and tickled it with a timothy straw until it hopped away.

As I walked on, I noticed a funny little bird running along in front of me. It would fall over on the ground, then kick and flutter around like it was crippled and dying. Each time I ran to help, but it would take off running ahead of me, doing the same silly act.

I got so tickled by this little bird that I had to stop to

catch my breath. The silly little creature just turned around and looked disappointed in me. Then it flew right over my head, landed square on the trail, and fell over on its back again, fluttering around.

I started to remember Dad talking about a little long-legged Mama Bird that would pretend to be crippled in order to lead other creatures away from her nest, protecting her eggs or baby birds.

A small log at the edge of the trail looked like a good place to rest. I ignored the Mama Bird and looked instead at the bare ground in front of me, where I had spotted two big, round-backed, black bugs pushing a monstrous ball of horse manure around with their hind feet. They were walking backwards—I guess they couldn't stand the smell of it.

Oscar and Dad had explained that these giant black bugs hide their eggs inside of that manure ball.

"That is why our corn grows so big and tall," Oscar had told me, "because thousands of these black bugs, called tumble bugs, push their balls of horse dung into our corn fields, then get lost and tired and leave them behind."

"That enriches the soil," Dad added, "and that makes everything grow a lot larger."

"Is that why you sold our manure spreader, Oscar?" I asked. I couldn't understand at my young age, why they laughed at things like this that I said. To me it was a pretty good question, but often Dad or Oscar just said, "Harold, you take the cake." That always puzzled me too, because there was *never* any cake to take when they said this.

Watching these tumble bugs closely, I laughed like kids laugh at cartoons today. They would get all mixed up in their directions, and each bug would decide that home was in a different direction. They worked on opposite sides of the manure ball, pushing with all of their might and getting absolutely nowhere.

Reluctant to leave this miniature comedy show, I slowly walked on down the path. I thought, "What friendly creatures I have around me, and how beautiful and captivating life is." I believed that it could stay this way for me forever, if only I never had to go inside a school again.

|54|

VOICES IN THE WOODS

Down at the Whitewater River, I tried to remember why I had come down here. With so many entertaining diversions, I had lost my train of thought.

Nearby I spotted a ten-foot-long seasoned willow pole, very light, just right for fishing. Then it dawned on me that I had wanted to see if the big catfish were starting their nesting period under the rock ledges. These huge ledges were about eight to twelve feet under the water where Pipe Creek joined with the big Whitewater River, and I wanted to dive down near the bottom to see if the catfish had arrived yet.

Suddenly, I heard some voices in the woods across Pipe Creek. I didn't know who the voices belonged to, but I wasn't looking for company. I quietly crept a hundred feet or so, then turned off the trail to my right to reach the privacy of the thick trees along the creek.

The water here flowed still and deep, and the big rock ledges lay about in the middle, under a lot of dangerous water. This water was about one hundred and thirty feet wide. To my surprise, I saw that a large live sycamore tree had fallen from the far bank of the channel. The sycamore was lying on the water with its top not more than forty feet out from where I stood.

I sat down quietly under the cover of the foliage on my side of the creek. Not wanting to swim with strangers around, I took some fishing line from my pocket and tied it to the small end of the willow pole that I had found along the trail. Next, I took a small fishhook from my slouchy cap and tied it to the end of my twenty-foot line with a sinker attached near the hook. I retrieved a dead worm from a pocket of my overalls for bait. I was ready to fish.

I listened closely to the sounds coming from the far bank of the channel. I thought I recognized the voices of the two oldest Brown boys. I was kind of scared of them. They were eighteen and twenty years old, and their father gave my Dad a little trouble, like stealing eggs first and then chickens. We also spotted Mr. Brown taking our watermelons without asking. Then he started to make illegal moonshine whiskey, locating his still deep in the woods on my Dad's side of the property line. Maybe his idea was to divert blame if anyone found the apparatus.

The Browns were our distant neighbors, and they were very poor—living in a hollow in the woods in a little shack. They made their living selling their moonshine to anyone who wanted it. Nobody turned them in to the law because of the hard time they had providing for their family. I liked the kids that were closer to my age, but I didn't want these two older Brown boys to see me.

The two tall, stout Brown boys emerged from the woods at the far end of a fallen sycamore across Pipe Creek from me. I was glad I was well hidden.

One of them untied a big shaggy dog I hadn't noticed before from the sycamore. It was wearing a muzzle, and it looked sick. Of course, almost any dog looks a little sick when it has to wear a muzzle.

The two boys were arguing about something, and I could see they were drinking from a jug. One of them picked up a large-caliber pistol from a small cloth backpack on the ground. They disappeared with the dog and the gun back into the woods, still arguing loudly. I could see that they had left their small backpack and jug behind.

I tried desperately to hear and understand what they were saying, but it was hopeless. Soon I heard a loud bang. I wondered if they had shot the dog, or maybe if one of the brothers had shot the other one.

Before long they returned to the sycamore without the poor old dog, and I knew that he must have been sick with rabies like Gussy had been. That would have explained the muzzle the dog had been wearing.

One of the brothers was carrying the dog muzzle and the other was carrying the pistol. I was scared to move a muscle for fear they might see my movement, mistake me for a game animal, and shoot me. I peeked again and saw they were taking off their clothes and acting wild.

I was getting tired of lying in the half-crouched position that I was in, trying to see what they were doing. I just had to do something to change it.

Suddenly, a big fish grabbed the dead worm on my hook and took off before I could grab the pole. Pole, line, and all zipped straight out into the open water. My big fish jumped and flopped right alongside the downed sycamore limbs, and then it headed straight toward the two Brown boys. The boys were standing on the far shore, pointing and yelling.

The channel cat was diving to the bottom and then jumping high into the air again and again.

This diversion gave me a good chance to move around and change the position of my aching body. The Brown boys were putting on quite a noisy show on the other side of this watery stage.

The big fish no doubt saw the arm-waving commotion of the excited boys. It turned sharply around and headed back at an angle toward my side. The Brown boys dove in and swam at top speed trying to catch it.

I was afraid that they would see me, so I got back down on the ground. I spotted a mass of wild grapevines hanging down into the water from the nearby trees to one side of me. I crawled slowly over to hide behind the hanging vines to keep out of view. I could still see the thrashing swimmers well enough through the many small openings.

But then the catfish changed course again and headed straight for my hiding place, pulling my pole only about thirty feet ahead of its pursuers. The big fish was holding its lead, and I think the brothers were tiring some.

I was rooting for the catfish, and telling him in a very quiet voice to hurry and escape. He seemed to respond to my thoughts by picking up speed, but he chose to swim straight into my grapevine hiding place. Immediately the fishing line got all tangled up in the horseweeds and vines. The water boiled and the stems thrashed around violently as my imprisoned friend worked to spit up my undersized hook. He made quick work of it, then raced away for deep water.

The Brown boys saw the big commotion in the horseweeds, and even though they were very tired, they finally reached my side of the bank.

By then, I had disappeared from there. I watched from a new hiding place as they stood in waist-deep water, tearing the grapevines to bits. They looked under every limb and twig for that elusive catfish.

They swam halfway back across Pipe Creek to the middle of the big floating sycamore, where they climbed up onto the trunk. They rested there for a long time, then got up and walked awkwardly along the trunk of the tree, heading toward where their clothes lay draped over their jug.

They pulled out some sandwiches and ate some, and took more drinks from their jug. They sat for awhile, and then when they tried to get up, they could hardly walk.

One boy offered the other another drink, but he pushed it away. They sat there for quite awhile and didn't touch the jug. They both looked sad and miserable.

|55|

SECRET RESCUE

After awhile the two Brown boys managed to get to their feet, and started to walk back out on the floating sycamore tree trunk. As they moved closer to the middle of the deep channel, they talked and pointed down into the water so I could guess they were talking about the big ledges of rock underwater.

Soon the younger boy slid from the tree trunk into the water and went under. He was gone a long time, and the older boy started to look very nervous and got into the water to look for his brother. Suddenly, there was a lot of splashing in the water out toward the top of the fallen sycamore, about thirty or forty feet from where I was watching.

The Brown boy who had gone into the water first was hanging on to an underwater limb of the tree, with only his nose and part of his face up out of the water. A huge Mississippi yellow catfish had a death grip on his other hand. The monstrous fish pulled the boy under the water at short intervals, while the boy fiercely hung onto the sycamore limb with his free hand.

The other boy scrambled back up on the trunk of the tree and moved toward him, yelling for his brother to hang on, but the big fish wrestled his brother loose and took him down to the bottom of Pipe Creek. The older boy on the sycamore slid into the deep water in search of his drowning brother.

Scared, I could no longer simply stand by and watch. Trying to keep my wits together, I ran up the trail hollering for help. I quickly realized that this was meaningless, since there was no one within a mile of that place.

"I am a good swimmer and diver," I said to myself. "I'll try to pull that boy out of the water."

I turned around, ran back, tore off my clothes, and jumped feet first into that chilly creek. Treading water for a couple of seconds, I thought about how I would have to dive under with the determination of a hardened lifeguard. I knew I was little, but very good in the water, whether on the surface or deep down at the bottom.

I flipped my feet high up in the air and headed straight down. I could feel the pressure mount as I went deeper. I reached the rocky ledge quickly with my eyes wide open in the clear water.

In seconds I searched the ledges and spotted the two boys. The big fish still had a grip on the hand of the younger boy, who seemed to be lifeless. The older boy was having a hard time getting his brother and the big fish to the surface, so I grabbed a hold of the his long brown hair and kicked vigorously, using every ounce of my strength to pull him up. We surfaced about six or seven seconds after and the boy managed to grab a tree limb with his free hand. He dragged himself out onto the trunk, still holding his drowning brother tightly by the arm.

Together we tugged and pulled the unconscious younger brother over the tree trunk feet first with his face down. The huge fish still held onto the boy's bleeding hand, and began to struggle again and cause more damage. The unconscious boy was already in a very good position for pumping the water from his lungs, and together his brother and I did what we could. After we pumped a lot of water from him, he started to cough and regained consciousness.

Then the older boy raced for his pistol and shot the huge fish in the head, making it relax so we could work the younger brother's hand from its mouth. His hand was lacerated on both sides.

The older boy returned the pistol to the small backpack and ran back out on the fallen sycamore trunk. He jumped in the water and swam to shore towing the big fish. On the shore he grabbed the jug and returned to give it to his brother. While the younger boy gasped and drank a couple of belts, his brother quickly cleaned the fish. The channel cat must have weighed close to ninety pounds.

Seeming to feel better now after sipping on the moonshine, the younger brother got to his feet. We helped him back to shore, and both of the Brown boys got dressed. I swam back to the other side.

"I sure am glad your brother was saved," I yelled to the older boy while getting dressed myself.

"I am too," he agreed. "We came real close . . . " His voice trailed off.

"I have got to get home now," I said, "before my whole family is all over the hills looking for me!"

"Who are you?" he yelled over the creek to me, looking at me as if he had just seen me for the first time.

"I am John Henry Hannebaum's youngest son, and I was hid behind all those grapevines fishing and watching you guys," I replied. "That was my catfish you were chasing when you first got into the creek."

The older Brown brother got real serious.

"I would sure like it a lot," he said, "if you wouldn't say a thing about what you heard or seen here today. 'Cause if my folks knew their favorite son damn-near drowned, they would kill me. They may kill me, anyway, when they see how bad his hand is chewed up."

This really scared me. "I will never say a word to anybody. I promise," I yelled.

I ran most of the way home, only to get a whipping from Mom for being gone so long and for not letting anybody know where I was going.

A couple of days later, Dollie went to get our mail. When she got back, she told Dad she had seen a jug of what looked like moonshine in the weeds right behind our mailbox. Dad saved it to give to my Uncle Doc as a coming-home gift when he got out of the Navy. I knew it was a gift from the oldest Brown boy—the most valuable thing he had to offer—but I didn't say anything.

When Uncle Doc finally came home Dad gave him the jug, but I figured he didn't like it because of the awful faces he made whenever he took drinks from it. He would pound his chest, cough, and make all kinds of other funny noises after each drink.

This is the first time I have told the story of the events of that first day of summer vacation since it happened many years ago.

|56|

MOM'S AWAY, WE PLAY

One beautiful Indiana summer morning Mom boarded the train at Connersville, heading back to see her brother Scott in Idaho. It had been a little over a year since their last visit together.

I wanted to go with Mom, but Dad said, "You are a young man of almost eight now, and I want you here with me. I need you for a fishing partner."

Soon we got a letter from Mom. It was so long that it took Dad almost three days to read it all.

"I wonder," Dad said, "how she can afford all the pencils, paper, and two-cent postage stamps for such a huge letter?" Dad looked at us with a twinkle in his eye. "She could have saved a lot of money by crating this letter and shipping it by freight."

I had a lot of fun fishing with Dad, Oscar, and Lester, so I didn't have time to miss Mom too much. One day, Dad took us fishing on Lockery Creek, about forty miles from home.

We camped by the creek for one day and night, then moved about ten miles downstream where we made another camp for a couple of days. Only then did I discover I had left my fishing pole, with the line still in the creek, back at our first camp.

"If you use the trail by the creek," Oscar said, "it's only about five miles back to our first camp. You can walk there and get your pole." Dad agreed with Oscar.

Me and Lester packed a lunch and started running up the trail along the creek. This was wild country for Indiana. In those days nobody lived near Lockery Creek.

Along the way we caught a lot of fish with Lester's line and pole. We left the fish we caught in the water on strings, and marked the places with dried horseweed stems so we could find them and pick them up on our way back to camp. We didn't think much about the return trip making a total of *ten* miles for us to walk.

We fooled around fishing and looking at a lot of interesting things along the trail. It was about sundown when we finally arrived at our first camp.

We were excited to find my fishing pole floating way out in deep water. We knew I had caught a big fish. Lester swam out and retrieved my pole, and I waded in, too, expecting a big fight. Instead, only a fish skeleton was left attached to my hook. Those darn crawdads had eaten our big catfish, and we were mad.

It was cold that night. Our wet clothes wouldn't dry, and we darn-near froze. We didn't have any matches, there was no moon, and we were scared in the pitch dark. We talked about maybe walking back down the creek, but it was so dark we couldn't even see our hands before our eyes.

We held onto each other to keep from getting separated and lost. I didn't realize that a night could get so dark. The skies thundered and there were many other strange noises all around us. We were terrified.

After awhile, we started to hear a noise that wasn't strange at all—it was the sound of the Maxwell's engine! The headlights soon showed through the trees and Dad and Oscar jumped out of the Maxwell at our old camp. They were awful glad to find us, rather than having us lost somewhere off the road and down the creek.

They started a fire which felt good to Lester and me. When we were warm and almost dry, the rain started to pour down. Oscar and Dad quickly put up the top on our Maxwell. We all piled in and headed for home. We decided we had had our fill of fishing and camping.

About a mile down through the woods, the car started steering badly. Oscar stopped, put on his raincoat, and found a low front tire with a nail in it. He changed the tire in the rain and mud.

We crossed three rising creeks that Dad said would swim a cow, milk and all, and didn't arrive home until early the next morning—cold, hungry, and dog-tired. A touring car in those days offered very little protection from the rain. Even with the top up, it would let in the wet and cold—especially in the back seat, where the windshield provided little or no shelter for Lester and me.

Back in our own beds at home we slept like dead people. But it wasn't long before Oscar and Dad began making plans for new expeditions.

"We will go fishing real soon down on the Whitewater River below Brookville," Oscar said, pointing out the spot on a map.

"No, Oscar," I said, "let's go fishing in Metamora."

"There are no fish there," he snorted. "In the Whitewater below Brookville there are a lot of big bass."

"Don't you remember, Oscar, those big ol' catfish that me and Omar caught in Metamora and had on ice there?" I asked. "Remember, I brought them home on the school wagon?"

"I recall one very large fish," Oscar admitted, "but only

half of one, and somebody had to have given it to you."

"No," I said, "me and Omar caught it. I had to give half of it to him and I brought my half home. We caught more big fish than just that one, too."

Oscar just nodded absentmindedly and didn't pay any attention to my suggestion. He really didn't like to fish with a pole much and refused to go to Metamora to fish.

Dad, however, listened and believed what I had told Oscar, and soon he took Lester and me to Metamora to fish.

The depot man wouldn't let us fish through their toilet holes anymore, so instead we threw our lines into the canal outside, letting our bait drift with the current twenty or thirty feet under the depot. Dad was always a better fisherman than we were, and before long he hooked a big one.

Me and Lester never saw Dad having such a good time before. He lost his pipe because he was talking and laughing so much.

"You can expect almost anything," he said to nobody in particular, "when you are out fishing with these darn kids of mine!"

It took Dad about ten exciting minutes to land a big channel cat, and in no time the whole population of Metamora was there. Dad had laughed so loud when he hooked onto his big fish that people nearby heard him, and the word quickly got around.

These townspeople never dreamed that big fish could be found under the old bridge and four or five buildings that had been built over the canal in downtown Metamora. Soon the canal was lined with fishing poles and happy fishermen.

Dad's fun really made us very happy. We had seldom seen our Dad have such a good laugh like that, and he was still having the time of his life.

"I probably hooked the only fish under there," he said to the natives of the town, but soon other fishing poles were flipping back and forth with big catfish.

When we arrived home with Dad's fish, we stopped by our mailbox and found a letter from Mom. We could tell she was getting homesick.

She wrote that she would soon be packing for home, after Scott and Ella took her on a trip in their Buick the next day. They planned to visit Hagerman Valley, then come back to Shoshone Falls, where they would cross the Snake River on a ferryboat made just for taking cars across above the falls.

"I will write to you again about our trip," she finished, "and let you know when to pick me up in Connersville."

About one week later, we got another letter from Mom. She said she would leave Idaho in two days and would let us know by telephone when to pick her up at Connersville. She planned to stay there overnight because the train would arrive late in the evening.

Mom also wrote about the evening when they crossed the Snake River on the ferry near Shoshone Falls. There was only one small dam on the Snake River then, and the water was still very deep. Four cars were driven onto the ferryboat, including Scott's Buick, which was at the rear.

Just as the loading was finished, a big black Cadillac drove up with four well-dressed businessmen in it. One of the men jumped out and began to talk urgently with the boatman and owner of the ferry.

"This ferry already has a full load on it," the boatman told them. "It will be a one-hour wait before I can take you gentlemen and your car over."

This news made the four men downright furious. They demanded that they be taken across or they would miss a very important meeting in Boise.

"I'm very sorry," said the boatman, "but I'm already overloaded and cannot oblige you."

At that point a lot of money started changing hands, maybe hundreds of dollars.

"Get out of your car and I will put her aboard—at your risk," the boatman said.

The boatman drove the heavy Cadillac aboard with its lights on, then got out and kept the ignition key. There was barely enough room behind the Buick for the big long Cadillac. The boatman hooked a rope across the ferry and tied it behind the car. He pulled it tight, then blocked one of the back wheels.

Mom wrote:

"The ferry was riding very high out of the water at the far

end and sat at a steep angle. The deck was, at times, awash.

"It was getting darker now. Just when we were all aboard, ready to go across, something snapped, and the big Cadillac started rolling. The block skidded out from under the back wheel and across the slick deck. The backward rolling Cadillac hit the rope and broke it without even slowing down. It toppled from the steep deck into the wild Snake River, and quickly sank.

"The Cadillac settled to the bottom on its back end, seventy feet down, with its headlights still on and pointing up at us. In the dark, clear waters of the river we could see it very plainly.

"The ferry leveled up, and we went on across to the north side. Those well-dressed gentlemen gambled and lost a lot of money and a very expensive car.

"I heard one of the men say, 'The only thing we can do now is to make a phone call to Boise, report that we lost our car in the Snake due to an accident, and then find out how many of our heads will roll—if any.'

"We never did learn whether they got their car out of that deep water," Mom finished.

We got one more letter from Mom from Idaho, saying she had been detained for three extra days. We were happy to have the extra time—our house was a mess because Mrs. Milbourne had not been feeling well. We took a vote to see who should clean it up. The vote was unanimous in favor of all of us cleaning together, so when Mom arrived home she wouldn't just turn around and leave again.

|57|

THE RETURN OF MOM

In three days, we got Mom's telephone call from nearby Connersville.

"Hello, world traveler," Dad said when he answered the

phone. In those days anyone who traveled more than a hundred miles from home was considered to be a world traveler.

"What hotel are you staying in?" he asked. Mom told him and Dad drove up to Connersville that evening, arriving just before midnight. He tapped on her locked door.

"Who is there?" Mom asked without opening the door.

"I am a baby buggy salesman," Dad said in a well-changed, fictitious voice. "Would you be interested in a couple of buggies, or in a single, rich and prosperous, double-muscled man for the night—or longer?"

Mom threw something against the door.

"Get out of here, you hooligan!" she shouted. "I have a baby buggy and I certainly don't need any more babies."

Dad was pleased with her reaction, until Mom opened the door slightly and said, "Come on in, honey. You can't fool me with that little accent you have. But I meant what I said about babies."

Mom and Dad were home by noon the next day. We welcomed them by playing "Home Sweet Home" on the Cecilian record player, with Arlie Rust playing along on his harmonica. Everyone rushed around and did a lot of hugging and handshaking.

Before they went inside, Dad took Mom around to show her a special coming-home present he had bought for her. It was a brand new motorized washing machine. It was powered by a little gas engine that we had attached to it. Mom was delighted at the thought of how much work our new invention would save both her and Mrs. Milbourne.

"I am glad that Mrs. Milbourne has kept the house so clean," exclaimed Mom, as she looked around through several rooms.

"Mrs. Milbourne is sick in bed," Dollie said, without telling her who had really done the cleaning.

Mom hurried into Mrs. Milbourne's room, and then called Dr. Cupp on the telephone. Dr. Cupp arrived soon in his Grant Six automobile. He gave her a checkup, then came out of her room.

"She must have rest," he told us, "and she must take these

pills as directed. She is in good health, for being eighty-six, but she is just plain worn out. Let her do only light work, if she feels like it, after she rests in bed for a few days."

Dr. Cupp was right. In a week or so Mrs. Milbourne was on her feet and feeling fine. She even felt good enough to go and see her grandkids.

With Mrs. Milbourne away, big-hearted Ol' Oscar watched over us kids. One day he came home with a book that he had bought called *Brewster's Millions*. He read it out loud to us. This book caused a lot of commotion in our family and we talked for months and months about it.

It was about a poor man named Brewster without a dollar to his name. Another man, a millionaire several times over, made a deal with Brewster. He said, "I will give you a million dollars cash, but you must invest it in something that will lose money. In fact, *you must lose the entire million dollars in one year*, but you can't hand it out to other people for nothing and you can't burn it. You must lose it only by investing it in anything you wish. If you can invest the first million and come up completely broke at the end of the year, I'll give you a million dollars of your very own to keep."

No matter how hard Brewster tried to invest in bad companies or to make other bad investments, he only made money! At the end of the first year he had to report that he had made a profit from the first million dollars and he had to give it all back. Once again he was a very poor man.

Oscar made it a game for our whole family to watch the investment pages of the newspapers. We searched high and low for stock investments that would lose a person a fortune. For months each of us kept careful records on how much, if any, of our imitation money we could lose. Oscar kept his record up to date the longest, showing the greatest interest. This fun game gave Mom some extra time for herself, and it gave Oscar a lot of new ideas about how one could make money by investing in the markets.

|58|

SMOKING BULLETS

We all agreed that a little party would be in order for Mom after she returned from Idaho. I was hoping a party would make her so happy that she wouldn't ever want to leave us again.

Dad must have felt the same way. I heard him tell one of our neighbors that he was trying to figure out how to keep Mom at home. "Getting her in the family way would do it," said the neighbor.

Later I asked Dad, "What does *family way* mean?"

"It means, Harold," Dad explained, "that a new little baby would be in our family." I couldn't understand how a helpless little baby could keep Mom home when *we* couldn't.

My three Jones uncles and Grandpaw and Grandmaw Jones were at the party, along with a keg of hard cider. Dad and Doc tried some of the cider and then decided to go hunting.

"We are going out in the woods to shoot some squirrels for supper," Dad told Mom.

"Okay," Mom said, "but be extra careful. You shouldn't have tasted that cider."

Dad slipped a few twenty-two shells into his pants pocket as he went outside.

Dad had his twenty-two rifle, and Uncle Doc carried the same twenty-two Browning Automatic that he had used when he almost blew up a mountain near Custer, Idaho.

After they had walked through the woods for awhile, Dad loaded up his pipe from his pants pocket where he kept his loose smoking tobacco, lit up, and started puffing away while he carefully squinted up into the tall trees looking for squirrels.

Dad spotted a big red squirrel in a tree, and, seeing that Uncle Doc was a short distance to his left and safe, he took careful aim at the squirrel. Suddenly there was a loud bang, and Dad's clay pipe was blown to bits leaving only the stem still in his mouth.

The red squirrel disappeared through the high tree limbs. Dad, with a look of astonishment on his face, pulled the pipe stem out of his mouth and examined it. Then he glared at Doc standing nearby and asked, "Did you shoot my pipe just to make me miss that squirrel?"

"Of course not," Doc said, looking surprised himself. "I didn't fire my gun at all. You fired your rifle, but you missed the squirrel. Your bullet must have ricocheted back somehow and miraculously hit your pipe."

"That seems impossible," Dad said, shaking his head. "But it must have happened that way."

Later they came home carrying six squirrels. Dad told us the story about his clay pipe being blown to bits, leaving only the stem clenched between his teeth. Everybody had a big laugh. It was hard for Dad to put that story across, because he didn't half believe it himself.

Oscar had a different idea.

"There must have been someone out there behind a tree," he said, "who took a potshot at you. Maybe it was Ol' Whiskey Brown getting even with you for putting that birdshot in his rear end for stealing our chickens last year."

We all considered Oscar's idea, and we were a little scared at the thought of someone shooting at Dad.

The next day, after Mom's party, Dad, Mom, and Oscar decided to try out the new power washing machine. Almost everyone gathered around outside to watch the fashionable new washing machine and its little gas engine do such a good job of washing its very first batch of our clothes.

Dad had his new clay pipe in his pocket, and as he talked he pulled it out and loaded it up with loose tobacco, lit it up, and started puffing away. He was still talking with Mom and Oscar between puffs when suddenly there was a loud bang. Once again, Dad's clay pipe had been blown to bits.

Everybody scattered for cover. Dad's right eye was hurt, and he looked around as best he could to see if Uncle Doc was there. He was a little suspicious that Doc might be shooting at his pipe again, but when he was sure that wasn't the case, he called for Doc so he could get some medical attention.

Mom quickly took Dad into the house. Doc wasn't there yet, so Mom carefully removed some tobacco particles from Dad's eye, along with one tiny piece of the clay pipe. She could see that the damage was not too serious.

Dad was fuming mad.

"Now, this is the second time in less than twenty-four hours for this very same thing to happen. What in the devil is going on?" He groaned but didn't talk while Mom continued to wash his eye. When she was finished, he stood with a wet cloth over his right eye and declared slowly and with great feeling, "I am going to get the dad-ratted yellow-bellied prankster who did this and commit murder on him, even if it takes me around the world and forever!"

I heard every word he said, and shivered, glad that it wasn't me who had anything to do with these mysterious shootings.

We all gathered in the house to watch Uncle Doc put a patch on Dad's right eye. With his patch on, Dad reminded us kids of the old pirates on the high seas that we had studied about in school. All Dad needed now was a wooden leg and a hook at the end of his arm. In fact, we were quite proud of Dad because even though his pipe had been shot to bits twice, he had not been hurt badly.

Oscar reported that he could find no strangers in our neighborhood, and soon we all went outside again. We circled around the washing machine to see how our clothes were being washed. Mom was going through some more clothes, getting them ready for the next washing.

After a few minutes, Mom called Dad over and showed him several small twenty-two caliber rifle shells that she had found mixed in with the loose tobacco in his pants pockets.

"Do you think the shells could have gotten into your pipe when you were filling it from your pocket?" she asked.

Dad took a good look at the loose tobacco in the pocket of the pants he was now wearing, and, to his surprise, he found two more of the small twenty-two shells mixed in. A funny look came over his face as he realized that this was the way his pipes had been blown up.

"It is very costly and also very dangerous," Mom lectured

him sternly, "to smoke ammunition with your tobacco." Then she looked at him with a smile. "You may need to order armor-plated pipe bowls from Montgomery Ward for your own protection."

|59|

WILD MUSCADINE GRAPEOVER

Now that Mom was home and the party over with, and Dad had no more clay pipes to blow up, we all thought a little peace and quiet would come to our family. That was when Mom looked out of our kitchen window and saw a mysterious man dressed in black tying up his horse and buggy to our hitch rack out back.

He came up to our door, but before he could knock, Mom guessed by the clothes he was wearing that he was the new preacher, and she let him in.

Mom was busy preparing our supper, so she escorted him into our parlor where she introduced him to Dad, who was sitting there in near darkness, nursing his patched eye.

They talked for awhile and soon started telling jokes about preachers. Then Dad discovered that he had met this man before, and they talked about some of the good times they used to have.

Presently, the preacher asked Dad about his patched eye, and how he had hurt it, because he didn't remember it from before.

Dad didn't want to talk about his eye and about how it had happened, so he smiled and said, "Oh, it is a long story and it happened a long time ago. I was a messenger boy in the Civil War, and I got this in the Battle of Chickamauga." He told the story of the Battle of Chickamauga just like he had heard it from Grandpaw Jones, who *had* been there.

"John, I can hardly believe it," exclaimed the preacher when Dad finished his story. "You don't look that old!"

"Well, I can hardly believe you can't believe me!" Dad answered with a grin.

The two men just sat there, wondering whether either one could believe the other.

"I will begin church services this Sunday at the little white church at Elm Grove," the preacher said, breaking the silence. "I would like you and your family to be there."

"You have my word," Dad promised, "but frankly, I can hardly believe you are old enough to be a preacher!"

"I can hardly believe you can't believe it!" replied the preacher with a big smile, and they both laughed.

The preacher got up to leave. He shook hands with Dad, then turned and bowed to Mom.

"Mrs. Hannebaum," he said to Mom purposefully, "it has been a great pleasure to visit in your home. Your kitchen is perfumed better than any other I have ever smelled."

Mom got the hint and said, "You must stay for supper!"

"God bless you! You are so very kind," he said, accepting.

Mom was anxious for everything to go smoothly and be perfect for the preacher. She even seated him at the head of the table in Dad's place.

The meal went very well and when it was nearly over, Mom decided that she wanted some special dessert for the new preacher. She went to the cellar and brought back a gallon jar of canned wild grapes. She had prepared them two years before, for just this sort of an occasion. This was the first jar, in fact, that she opened.

The mixture of wild grapes was mostly all juice. Mom sampled it and said, "Nothing ever tasted so good. I'm glad I thought of these wild grapes." She put the grapes in fruit dessert dishes and put them on the side table until everyone was finished.

Soon the preacher said, "The dessert, Mrs. Hannebaum, has an overwhelmingly pleasant and appetizing smell. What is it?"

"Those are canned wild muscadine grapes," Mom said, serving them. "I put up ten gallons of them about two years ago. Eat all that you like—we have plenty more."

The preacher had eaten a light meal, apparently saving up

for dessert. He enjoyed several large bowls of grapes.

"These wild grapes are so *delicious*," he exclaimed. "I don't believe I have ever eaten canned wild grapes before."

Everyone was glad that the preacher was enjoying the meal and Mom gave him still another dish of grapes.

Mom didn't realize that her wild muscadine grapes had fermented in the jar and had, in fact, become a very strong wine. They were probably about fourteen or fifteen percent alcohol.

The poor preacher man was now becoming intoxicated. Mom thought he was having a mild dizzy spell from overeating or perhaps from eating too fast. She even considered that he might be suffering a relapse of some unknown disease from his past.

"Honey," Dad whispered to Mom, "I think it is the alcohol in your wild grapes that makes them taste so good. Your dessert is really a very strong wine."

Mom was so embarrassed that she just sat there for a few minutes.

"We must not let the preacher drive his horse and buggy home until he sobers up," Dad whispered to Mom. "In fact, as late as it is now, we should put him to bed until morning."

Dad and Oscar helped the very intoxicated preacher into the downstairs bedroom, where he slept all through the night with his clothes and shoes on.

Arlie, unbeknownst to anybody else, put the preacher's horse in a stall in our livestock barn where he fed and watered it, and then he put the shiny buggy in our carriage house.

The next morning, Mom and Dad explained to the confused preacher that he had accidentally eaten too many of the wild muscadine grapes, which are by nature a sleeping agent. The extreme dizziness and drowsiness, they explained, had the same effect on the wild animals and birds of the woods if they accidentally ate too many of the grapes.

The preacher acted very amazed at their knowledge of nature, but of course he knew what had really happened. He knew he had to act out a part with Mom and Dad to protect his reputation and the innocence of us kids. We could see that he felt good about how Mom and Dad had handled the situation.

The preacher emerged from our house squinting into the bright morning sunshine, expecting to see his horse and buggy waiting. When he saw they were missing, he became very confused. He turned and rushed back into the house, where he found Mom.

"I thought I left my horse and buggy at the hitch rack, but I can't seem to see them anywhere," he said nervously.

Mom walked to the window, pushed back the curtain and looked out. "There they are," she said smiling, "tied to the hitch rack just where you left them."

Arlie had risen early, harnessed the preacher's horse to the buggy, and with the timing of a magician, tied the horse to the rack just one moment before Mom looked out, then disappeared to do his other chores.

The preacher was totally confused now. Dad and Mom led him to the kitchen doorway and stood together at the top of our stone walkway while he made his trembling way toward his very visible horse and buggy. When he reached his rig, the preacher stretched both of his arms high over his head for a moment.

"He is probably thanking God for saving him from going blind and for delivering him from these strange people," Mom whispered to Dad. Dad had to turn and run into the house to muffle his laughter, and Mom followed him giggling. Soon everyone in our house was convulsed in muffled laughter.

Before long, Mom's ten gallons of canned wild grapes were completely used up by Dad and Oscar.

Many times during my youth we went to hear the preacher at his little white church at Elm Grove. Many times he had his feet under Mom's dinner table, but she never again served wild muscadine grapes to him, or to any of our other company who stayed for a meal.

|60|

FALLEN ANGELS

It thundered and rained all one Friday night, and when morning came me and Lester woke up to find it was rainy but warm—just the kind of Saturday weather we liked best.

We pulled on our faded overalls and carefully slipped away from the watchful eyes of Bert.

We ran down the trail beside Pipe Creek toward the Whitewater River, and soon the soft river mud was oozing up, friendly-like, between our toes.

As usual Lummox followed at his own speed, and when he arrived he flopped down to enjoy the sight and sound of high water.

The night-long rain really had the river on a rampage. The swift muddy waters made swimming look like more fun than ever. Before long we spotted a big log floating downstream, threw off our overalls, and swam like crazy until we reached the log.

I was small for my age, but very good in the water. We stood and sat on our giant log for a mile or so, having the most fun we had ever had in our young lives!

Ol' Lummox, still guarding our overalls, or at least sleeping by them, disappeared far behind us. Now I wondered if he would get sick of all of this rain and wander home alone. That would be bad for us, because then our folks would send out a search party.

Suddenly in a very swift spot our log struck a huge submerged rock, rolled over, and dumped us off right into the worst part of the raging waters!

We tried to swim for shore but the current washed us violently downstream. I lost track of Lester in the high waves, but I wasn't worried. He always seemed to show up after close calls. I tried to make my way toward shore, even if it was on the wrong side of the river.

I finally grabbed hold of some tree roots and weeds when I drifted close to a steep bank. I was very lucky to get out alive.

After I got my breath back, I climbed up the steep bank and sure enough, there was Lester a ways back, standing on the other side of the river. He was waving his arms and yelling something. I couldn't hear him because of the roaring waters, and I couldn't understand his monkey motions either.

Now I was scared for the first time. I knew it would take us a long time to get home, and that would worry Dad and Mom an awful lot. We were sure to get a thrashing from them.

The Whitewater River averaged about one hundred and fifty feet wide. Today it was running extra deep and swift. I knew I had to get back to the right side of the river before my older brother decided to swim over to help me. Even if he made it over in the swift current, both of us would still be on the wrong side, naked and hungry. I figured if I waited too long, he would feel like he had to come save me.

I thought back to when I had helped one of the Brown boys rescue his younger brother. That had been only a year or so ago, when the younger boy had been held under the deep waters of Pipe Creek by a huge catfish. I took a quick look at Lester and figured that this situation was no worse than that one.

I sucked in a couple of deep breaths, and saw that Lester was still on the riverbank making sweeping gestures at me. Quickly I dove into the raging waters before I could change my mind.

For some reason I was not afraid and felt at ease in the swift river. About halfway across I maneuvered myself alongside the drifting remains of an old wooden rowboat and clung to it to rest for awhile.

Lester was running along a steep gravel bar trying to keep up with me. Suddenly the swift water slowed down, and I realized I was caught in the edge of a deep whirlpool. I waited until the twisting current carried me close to where he stood. He held out a very long willow pole as far as he could toward me. If I had missed the end of his long pole, I don't believe I would be writing this story today.

Now we were both on the right side of the river together! We were lucky that the summer rain was still warm as we plodded through the sticky mud toward home. We were probably a total of about two and a half miles away. We had to walk upriver to where Pipe Creek joined the Whitewater River and then down the trail. Every step of the way we knew we were sure to get a big thrashing from Mom and Dad.

We were both as naked as jaybirds and dripping all over with shiny river mud. When we reached the confluence of Pipe Creek and the Whitewater River, we couldn't find the place where we left our overalls—everything around was now underwater.

"Gee, Harold," Lester said with a big awful-looking grin, "You're sure ugly when you're naked—but you don't look bad where the mud is!"

"Golly, Les," I said, ignoring him, "we gotta go back downriver and see if we can find our clothes!"

"There's no use—the river has washed them away to China long ago. Lazy ol' Lummox probably watched them go without even barking when they floated off."

"Ya," I said, "and guess what will happen when he wanders on home without us." In silence we walked along for awhile.

"Gee, Lester," I said, as an awful thought hit me, "do you think we will be able to sit down to eat tonight, after we get our bare hind ends thrashed? Dad won't allow us to stand up anymore while we eat."

"I hadn't thought of that," Lester said, as our big problem began to sink in.

I felt better now that I could see Lester was giving his undivided attention to our hopeless predicament. It was then that Lester came up with the most brilliant idea I had ever heard in all of my young life. It made me proud to be his brother and to be able to learn deep thinking at his muddy feet.

"Harold, we're both hungry," he said, "but if we go home to eat we'll get thrashed for sure and probably get sent to bed without supper. Let's hole up in the tobacco barn until dark. We can eat some apples from Dad's winesap trees. We can put on some gunnysacks to keep warm and sleep overnight in the barn. Then by morning they'll be so happy to see us they won't hurt us—they'll probably give us a breakfast as big as a house!"

"Great thinking, Les!" I said, as a big smile spread all over my dirty face. I wondered if I would *ever* get to be as smart as Lester.

As the clouds of doom lifted and drifted away, another terrifying thought replaced all of my other worries: Crystal and Nolly Schankel! These two girls lived just down the road and often walked through these woods. Crystal was my "secret" girlfriend—but I was the only one who knew it.

"We must be awful dumb," I thought to myself, "to walk two or more miles naked through the woods, running the risk of some neighbor kids looking at us—especially Crystal and Nolly!"

So I kept a sharp eye out for any people who might see us, but luckily every living thing shunned us, even Lummox and his best friend, the neighbor's big-hearted rabbit hound.

While we waited for dark in Dad's empty tobacco barn, we found two empty gunnysacks that had once been full of hog feed for Oscar's hogs. We made leg holes in the bottoms and put them on. To our surprise, they were almost as warm as our overalls!

When it was good and dark, we crept out and ate a lot of green apples from Dad's winesap apple trees. It was so dark and we were so hungry that we didn't pay any attention to whether or not there were worms in the apples. We knew it would take lots of little apples to get us through our night alone.

"We should gather some hay together to sleep on in the barn," I said to Lester, as we munched on the sour and woody-tasting apples.

"That will be one of the first places they will look for us," said Lester, "and besides, I have a better idea."

Our bellies were feeling a bit woozy, but we were too busy to pay much attention. We worked hard inside the pitch-black tobacco barn. Feeling our way blindly, we found a lot of five-foot-long hardwood tobacco sticks and carried them up, placing them across the big timbers that ran just under the barn roof to make a platform. It would be warm and out of sight up in the rafters.

But the tobacco sticks were simply lying there loose and were not fastened down in any way. It was actually a very dangerous place to spend the night, especially since it was more than twenty feet up from the floor of the barn. We rested on our improvised bed, just testing it out.

"Say, did you feel something brush by your face?" Lester asked.

"Ya," I said, "don't get yourself all stewed to pieces—it's only Just Plain Cat. I reckon he probably wants to share our funny bed and maybe hunt sparrows here in the barn all night."

Lying there in the silence—broken by our growling stomachs—I felt warm and happy, dreaming about a breakfast as big as a house! I guess I dozed a little, and maybe turned over in my sleep on that punishing tobacco-stick bed.

Suddenly I heard a few of the tobacco sticks clatter to the floor of the barn. It sounded like gunfire!

Before I knew it, I hit the ground, too! More tobacco sticks came falling down on top of me. Lummox yelped and I felt his soft fur. I know Just Plain Cat fell, too, because he yowled all the way down and gripped his claws good into my bony legs when he landed!

Lying there with the wind knocked right out of me, I couldn't make a sound, and couldn't hear anything except my heart pounding loudly in my head. After a bit, I heard Lester's drawling voice up in the rafters.

"Harold, if you needed to use the toilet, why didn't you just *climb* down instead of jumping?"

I was beginning to get my air back a little, and I started to cry. It was awhile before I could answer Lester.

"I fell!" I gasped. "I wasn't needing to go to the outhouse, and I don't need to now!"

"Is Just Plain Cat okay?" Lester asked.

"Better than me," I replied weakly. "But I think I fell on Lummox. Looks like he just rolled over and went back to sleep."

I stayed there on the barn floor, trying hard to keep Lester from hearing me crying. I carefully moved one leg and then the other one. I found that everything was fine, except for my being bruised and skinned up some. I was still wearing my feed sack.

The heavy hardwood sticks kept falling from time to time. I was sure that Lester would fall next, but he never did. That was a lucky thing for me—I was lying directly under him!

Soon a dim light appeared at the far end of the big barn. We could hear one of the very large double doors as it glided open. It hung from a steel track about fourteen feet off the ground, and rumbled open smoothly on two sets of double rollers. A bright light appeared on the far side of the long platform scales that Dad used to weigh loads of tobacco.

"Don't make a sound!" I croaked weakly to Lester. "It's our folks!"

Everyone in the family was talking about the big noise they had heard coming from this area. I was lying at the far end of the big barn about one hundred feet from them.

Dad was carrying his ten-gauge shotgun and was swinging it wildly from side to side. Oscar held a lantern in one hand and a "sap," a thirty-two-caliber hammerless Bulldog brand pistol, in the other. Mom followed right behind them.

"Come out where I can see you!" Dad yelled loudly. "I'll give you what you need, but I'll *kill* you if you try to steal it!"

"*Don't be a fool!*" Oscar yelled. "Walk my way with your hands up!"

"I wish I could walk," I thought to myself, "Oscar's way or any other way, and then I wouldn't have to lie here on my back, choking for breath and waiting for them to finish me off!"

They were still slowly coming our way waving their guns inside a big bright ring of lantern light. Then I guess Mom heard me crying and came running to me.

"Where have you been, Harold?" she cried. "And where is Lester? Are you kids hurt?"

Boy, oh, boy, was I ever scared! I would have traded anything and everything I owned for a good alibi!

But I just laid there moaning and groaning and crying my little heart out. Mom wrapped her soft arms around me, and I felt so bad about the grief that Lester and I had caused our folks. Then we heard Lester's voice coming down from the rafters.

"Harold fell out of bed, Mom, and almost killed poor ol' Lummox." Lester began to spill the real story—he was incapable of telling a lie in the face of all of that firepower, particularly Mom's warm sympathy!

"Oh you poor little angels!" Mom said. She picked me up in her arms and carried me to the house. I felt as fluffy as a big white cloud as she carried me along.

Lester and Just Plain Cat followed along behind Mom. Lester and me both acted as dumb as we could, like we had no more brains than to hide out in the barn to avoid a big thrashing!

Mom stood in the middle of her kitchen holding something awful in her right hand under her apron. Lester and I spilled the whole story like we were as innocent as a dream while she questioned us as to where we had been all day before we hid out in the tobacco barn. Bert sat silently in one of the kitchen chairs, getting his licks in without saying a word.

"We have been looking for you at all of the neighbor's houses, in the woods, and, for the last ten hours, at the river, where you left a lot of your footprints." She looked very stern.

"Before you two get any clothes to put on," she said, "you will first get a thrashing from me, and then from your Dad, if he thinks you deserve more."

For the rest of that night we slept on welts. We had to stay in separate rooms all the next day, with only a cup of milk and one slice of homemade bread each.

The lessons that we learned were never forgotten. As I look back at the trying times that we caused my folks, I thank them—even Bert—for keeping us on the straight and narrow.

And through it all, I knew that Mom and Grandmaw still thought of us as "little angels"—even though we fell down on the job now and then.

|61|

A LITTLE DEEP THINKING

One day my Dad came into the house with a grim look on his face after a visit to our two-holer outhouse. He asked us all to gather around, then announced his complaint that we were using up the Montgomery Ward catalog far too fast. In those days the catalog was printed on softer paper that was well suited for privy paper.

"We are putting more paper than anything else through the holes," he said. "I would like to ask each one in our family to do a little deep thinking and give me your suggestions on how we can save paper."

Smart Ol' Lester was the first to raise his hand. "We can all quit going to the privy so much!" he suggested.

Bert added, "Why don't we all pitch in, load the privy on the big hay wagon, take it across yonder field and place it just this side of the Mofford brothers' fence. That way we won't use it so often, 'cause of it being so far away across the field, where the mean ol' bull is watching for us all the time."

I didn't like Bert's idea and said so, even though at the present location I had to face lots of abuse from our latest gang of mean roosters. I hated the idea of risking problems with a vicious bull.

Soon I had an idea and held up my hand. "Yes, Harold," Dad said, "what do you suggest?"

"I suggest that we take the meat saw from the meat house and saw the catalog in half—that should give us twice as many wipes!" I said, proud of my deep thinking.

"You kids all have good ideas," Dad admitted. "Lester's idea is a good one, but it has a fault. By not going to the privy when Mother Nature calls, it would cause us to spend more money for laxatives, thus using up more paper in the long run." He patted Lester on the shoulder, then turned to Bert.

"And Bert's idea is also good, but has some meager faults

as to the distance. But maybe a relocation halfway there would do the trick. The other fault is that our neighbor would then use it, since it would then be closer to his house than his own outhouse now is."

Dad finally settled on my idea as the best. He sawed the Montgomery Ward catalog in half and placed the second half in reserve until the first was gone.

|62|

DOLLIE AND THE AFTER-SNAP

Several days later, Dad and Oscar took Lester and me on a long walk beyond the confluence of Pipe Creek with the White-water River to a place we had never been before. Oscar carried a big empty sack.

"What are you going to use that big sack for?" I asked him.

"It's to put turtles in," Oscar said.

Along the way we saw a lot of soft-shell turtles, but when they heard us coming, they would run for the river and hide. We had no luck catching any of them.

Dad got out ahead of us and we saw him looking at something in a muddy area.

"Come here!" he hollered. "I want to show you something."

We hurried to where he was and he showed us some very large tracks. "Have you ever seen tracks that big?" We all shook our heads no.

"Those are the tracks of a very large snapping turtle," Dad said. "He must be a huge one. Looks like he is heading from the river through the weeds towards the swamp. We must hurry—we may be able to overtake him before he gets into the waters of the swamp."

Oscar cut a large forked limb from a tree, thinking he could use this to put over the turtle's neck, if we were lucky enough to overtake it.

We soon found the giant turtle in a small patch of thickly tangled swamp grass. Dad quickly got a small rope securely looped around his tail, and we dragged him backwards out of the grass.

"There is enough delicious meat here to feed us for a week or more," Dad said happily. "Harold and Lester, stay away from Mr. Snapping Turtle's head. He is very dangerous and unpredictable, and he can snap off one of your feet in one bite."

Oscar and Dad tried to put the turtle into the big bag, but he snapped at everything and made that impossible.

Oscar put his forked pole over the turtle's big neck to hold him, but that proved to be useless, too. The snapper was just too stout.

The only thing we could do was drag him by the rope to a nearby clump of willows, where we tied him to a willow tree.

Dad put a stout stick into the turtle's big open mouth, and the turtle bit down securely on it. Dad tied another rope to the stout stick and tied it to a different willow tree, stretching the turtle out as much as possible. He was now fairly secure and could not bite.

Dad and Oscar next carefully tied the big turtle's two hind feet together, then tied his two front feet together. They put an eight-foot-long pole between both front and hind legs.

The snapper had a death grip on the stick with his big mouth and we had a little trouble getting him to let go, but finally it splintered to pieces.

With Oscar on one end and Dad on the other end of the big pole, they picked him up, placed the pole ends on their shoulders, and we all headed home.

When we arrived, we turned the turtle loose on our well-fenced-in lawn. We all went to bed exhausted.

The next morning we found the turtle hiding under one of our rosebushes. Dad gave him a stick to bite and pulled his head out from under his shell. Then Dad cut the snapper's head off with a sharp ax and started butchering him.

We were all looking on and paying little attention to anything else. Dollie was very curious about the turtle's head, lying there on the lawn with its eyes and mouth wide open. She was barefooted, and she poked her right foot into the big open mouth. Suddenly it snapped shut.

She screamed in pain. Oscar and Dad quickly tried to pry the turtle's mouth open, but it would not budge.

Dad saw that Dollie was close to losing all the toes on her right foot except her little toe. Working fast, he grabbed the sharp knife he had been using to butcher the turtle and cut deep into the jaw muscles on each side of the turtle's head.

Finally the turtle's mouth relaxed, and Dollie was free. But she was still bleeding and crying from the pain. We quickly took her into the house, where Uncle Doc and Mom sewed up some of the cuts. Doc, using several medications, bandaged her foot.

Dollie was made to sit in an easy chair with her foot up for the rest of the day. Everyone showered her with lots of attention.

Uncle Doc and Mom watched Dollie very closely for two or three days for signs of infection. Blood poisoning and gangrene were both very common in those days. Many people lost their lives since there was no penicillin, no sulfa, and no other miracle drugs to combat infection.

"It is strange," Dad said to me, "how a turtle's jaw muscles will function long after his head has been severed from his body. And as far as I know, only a snapping turtle's head will do this."

Dollie used a cane to walk for several days. In a week or so, she was nearly as good as new, and in a month she was wearing her fancy high heels.

We found Henry Karns almost living with us during this time. I could tell he was in love with Dollie, and she liked him. This special attention helped Dollie to keep her spirits up while her toes returned to normal.

Henry took Dollie out many times in his beautiful black Saxon automobile. Sometimes they went to the picture show at Brookville. On other occasions, when Mom and Dad were there to watch, they enjoyed whirling around the floor at a dance, the snapping turtle and Dollie's near tragedy all but forgotten.

|63|

DOLLIE RUNS AFTER A LIGHTNING ROD SALESMAN

A man driving a one-horse spring wagon stopped at our front gate one day and tooted a funny little horn.

"When it rains, it pours," Dad said with a look of mild pain on his face. "I think I know this salesman from a ways back."

Dad went out to see what he was selling this time. They talked for awhile, and I watched with great curiosity from the window.

"What is he selling?" I asked Dad when he came back inside.

"Lightning rods," he said with a smile.

"Is that an awful fast stick of some kind for Mom to whip me and Lester with?" I asked with a shudder. It scared me just to think about a lightning-fast whip like that.

After a big laugh, Dad said, "Oh no, they have something to do with keeping lightning from hitting a building."

Now I was really puzzled.

Dad returned to continue talking with the salesman, and this time I went with him. I listened and looked over his wagon. The back end of the wagon was full of lightning rods, made from many sizes of pipes, all between four to six feet long.

The salesman was at our place all that day, desperately trying to explain to Dad how they worked and to persuade Dad how much he needed them.

"No," Dad kept saying, "lightning never did strike any of our buildings."

"What about your trees?" the man finally asked.

"At times," Dad admitted, "lightning did strike some of the big trees near our buildings."

Dad knew that it was dangerous to admit anything to a salesman, but he quickly thought of a comeback.

"I believe, however, that the tall trees keep my buildings from being hit," he said with a smile.

At this point the salesman pretended to give up. Before long, however, he was trying to sell Dad a new cross-cut saw and an ax to cut down the trees before the wind blew them down on top of our buildings. It didn't take us two seconds to realize that he was still trying to sell Dad those lightning rods.

This salesman was so determined to make a sale that he offered Dad a special deal. He offered his best lightning rods to put on the highest point of our big stock barn and on top of our two-and-a-half-story house, all at half of the regular price, with free installation. Dad's part of the deal was to tell prospective customers how the lightning rods worked and how they protected his buildings.

Dad finally agreed to this, but nothing was put on paper and signed. In those days people always trusted each other, and a man's word was as precious as life itself. If someone who broke his word ever did settle into the community, no one would do business with him and his days there were numbered.

With the help of Bert and Arlie, the salesman was busy for over six days installing both lightning rods and the heavy copper cables that ran from them down into the ground. They installed four lightning rods on our big livestock barn and four on our house roof. Mom was scared to death that someone would fall from those high roofs and break his neck.

We all gathered around while Dad paid the man with cash equal to half of the regular price. They shook hands with each other, and then the salesman drove off in his one-horse wagon.

To our surprise, Dollie followed, trotting along behind the wagon, not saying a word. She disappeared from sight down a slope in the road. After a moment we all ran down the road, too. We wanted to catch up with Dollie and the wagon to see why she was following it. When we caught up with them, the salesman had stopped and was standing near the back of his wagon talking to Dollie.

When we got closer we saw that she had gotten one of her fingers stuck in the bottom end of a hollow lightning rod in the wagon.

I ran back to the house for some warm, soapy water. We poured it down the open end of the rod and soon her finger was released.

Dollie, now seventeen, was so embarrassed that she said nothing, but ran back to the house crying. Dad saw how she felt, and he warned everyone, from Mom and Oscar right down to us kids, not to even mention the incident to anyone, and especially not to Henry Karns.

"You must treat Dollie as if nothing like this ever happened to her," he said.

Several times after that, Mom and Dad had to help Lester or me to get a finger or two loose from tight pipes where they were trapped. We were always freed by a snickering rescuer who showered us with sharp comments, and we certainly never got the royal treatment that Dad had demanded from all of us for Dollie.

LESTER DISAPPEARS

Oscar had heard a lot about the fine farmland and the good money that could be made in Idaho. These reports came from my Mom and from Uncle Scott's letters.

Oscar sold his half-interest in our Maxwell car to Dad and also sold off most of his purebred livestock. He was now well-fixed with money, and he purchased a brand new Oakland Roadster automobile from Joe Cashbaum in Brookville.

Me and Lester didn't think anything could take the place of our beautiful black Maxwell, but that dark green Oakland Roadster was a dream and was about all we could think about. We figured it could go a hundred miles an hour, but we told the neighbor kids that it could go two hundred miles an hour, and I think they believed us.

Oscar received several special letters from Idaho detailing land prices and annual weather conditions. He learned what crops grew best there and was told that the land had to be specially irrigated with water from the Snake River. Most of the buildings there, he found out, were "try-out" shacks of one or two rooms.

Oscar made a trip to Idaho to see for himself what the country was like. He saw a new frontier and a great future for a young, ambitious person. He bought a one-hundred-and-twenty-acre farm with a five-room house and several outbuildings for ten thousand dollars. Then he came back to Indiana and sold off the remainder of his holdings.

"Oscar, are you a millionaire yet?" I asked him.

"No," he replied, smiling. "I'm sorta like Brewster before anybody made any offers to him."

A few days later, Oscar said to Arlie, "I would like you to consider going to Idaho with me. I'll pay you to work for me."

"This is what I have always wanted," Arlie answered, smiling. "I have always wanted to take a trip out West."

Lester became determined to go out to Idaho, too, but nobody paid any attention to him. Lester was probably the most determined ten-year-old kid ever seen in Franklin County, Indiana.

"Please, can I go to Idaho with you and Arlie?" Lester pleaded again and again.

Oscar's answer was always the same.

"No, Lester, you must stay at home with Mom and Dad."

Arlie was about twenty now, and he had never in his life been more than ten miles from home. In fact, this was a giant step for all of us.

Oscar and Arlie got the new Oakland Roadster ready, including four spare tires strapped to the rear, for the trip of two thousand eight hundred miles.

With the Oakland ready to go, Oscar and Arlie came into the kitchen to have supper one last time with the rest of the family. We all ate quietly, each thinking our own thoughts. We were excited about their adventurous trip to Idaho, but sad because our family would soon be divided.

"Where is Lester?" Dad said, breaking the silence. No one knew, not even me.

"Maybe he is off fishing," Dollie guessed.

"Maybe he started off for Idaho," said Oscar, smiling.

"I think maybe he went to our tenant house," I said, "to see if Bender or Mr. Cummins left anything when they moved out awhile back."

That was something I had been intending to do. Dad had decided that he didn't want to grow any more tobacco for a year or two. He wanted to build his land up with hay and pasture. He offered to let the Cummins family live in our tenant house in the meantime if they wanted to. After doing some thinking and planning, however, they had decided to move.

When Lester was not home by dark, we all began to get worried about him. Mom knew how well he liked his supper. She started calling all of our neighbors on the telephone, asking them to watch for him.

By bedtime, Dad was very angry at Lester for worrying Mom and the rest of the family.

"I will tan his hide when he comes home," Dad said, "unless he has an awful good reason for doing this."

Well, Dad never had to tan Lester's hide, as he never did come home.

The next morning, Oscar and Arlie bid us a subdued goodbye and Oscar added, "We will look for Lester along the way."

Oscar started up the Oakland's engine, and they disappeared down the main gravel road toward Indianapolis, heading for Idaho, and leaving only a little cloud of dust in the air.

The day dragged on slowly, with everyone worried about Oscar, Arlie, and Lester, too.

That evening Oscar called Mom on the phone, and was very surprised to learn that Lester was still missing.

"There are a lot of people out looking for him now," Mom told him.

"We will call again later and see what's happening," Oscar said.

"Maybe I will have good news for you then," said Mom before she hung up with a shaky hand.

Oscar and Arlie made camp that night about seventy-five

miles west of Indianapolis. The next morning they called again, only to find out that Lester was still missing and that a dragnet operation had been started in our neighborhood. People were out looking through the wooded areas and creek, and especially searching around the Whitewater River.

I searched in the waters of Pipe Creek with Mom for a few miles in both directions from our place, but we couldn't even find any fresh tracks that might be Lester's. I looked carefully for a hollow horseweed stem sticking up out of the water in case he was hiding from us. Mom was so worried now that it was difficult for her to think. Lester was my best friend, clever and helpful to me, and I was scared for him.

That evening Oscar called us a third time. Mom had to shout into the telephone for him to hear. "There is no trace of him yet, but I *don't* want you to turn around and to come back home to look for him."

Our house was filled with people comforting Mom and reporting that there was still no news. The telephone rang constantly. Someone contacted the young preacher at the little white church at Elm Grove and he came by. It was very dusty around our house with everyone coming and going.

Late in the afternoon, Oscar and Arlie passed through a small town about three hundred and fifty miles from home. About a half-mile or so ahead of them they saw what looked like a small person walking along the side of the road. By the time they reached that spot, this person had left the road and was lying down resting by a small tree near a creek.

As they passed, Oscar said, "By golly, I can't believe my eyes, but there's Ol' Lester!"

"Damned if it isn't," Arlie said. "That *is* Lester, all right! I just can't believe it."

Oscar quickly stopped the car and backed it up. Lester had jumped up and was running after them, half crying and half laughing.

"Please, can I go to Idaho with you?" pleaded Lester, using the same words he had used many times at home.

Oscar quickly picked up the exhausted ten-year-old boy and lifted him up between Arlie and himself, then drove on.

"Let's find a phone and see if it's possible to get through

to Mom and Dad," said Oscar. "We must let them know that you are okay, and that you are here with us. Then we'll ask if they will let you go on to Idaho with us."

At the next town, Oscar finally got through to Dad on the telephone.

"Don't worry any more about Lester," Oscar told them. "We have just found him walking along the road, very determined to get to Idaho. In fact, he has come about three hundred and fifty miles completely on his own."

This was very hard for Dad to believe. Oscar had to repeat his message several times before Dad trusted his ears.

"Well, I'll be damned," Dad said softly. "That kid is one smart and determined cookie."

"You're right, Dad," Oscar agreed. "But what shall we do with him *now?* He still wants very much to go on to Idaho."

Dad thought for a minute or so, then said, "If it is okay with you and Arlie, take him along. He would only leave home again for Idaho if you brought him back."

"I think you are right, Dad," Oscar agreed.

"Oscar, if you think you can control him and you want him to go along, you can take him," Dad added, "or you will have to bring him back. The problem is now in your lap."

Oscar made his decision quickly.

"We will take him on with us and let you know how things go by letter since it is so hard to get through from Idaho on the telephone. Bringing Lester back would only delay us by several days, and those are days I don't want to lose."

|65|

WHAT HAPPENED TO LESTER

Back in the car again and on the road to Idaho for sure now, Lester told Oscar and Arlie about his trip from home.

"I didn't have to walk very much," he said, "because several buggies and a couple of cars gave me rides. Some of the people even gave me money to buy food with."

"How did you sleep at night?" Arlie asked him.

"One woman and a man gave me a blanket to sleep on. They told me that they would try to call my folks. They even tried to make me stay at their house. I told them, 'No, I can't stay. My brother Oscar will be along soon in his Oakland Roadster, and then I can ride with him to Idaho.' But it looked like they were dead set on keeping me with them."

"What did you do?" Oscar asked.

"I ran away from them, leaving their blanket behind. I was afraid they would send me back home and stop my trip to Idaho, but I did yell, 'Thank you for everything!' I left them about one hour ago or so, just before I found you."

Oscar started to laugh.

"*You* found *us?* We thought that *we* found *you*, and not that *you* found *us!*" He rumpled Lester's hair. "What matters most now, Lester, is that you are not lost anymore and neither are we."

They rode along without talking for awhile, thinking about the events of the day and their remarkable luck in getting back together.

"By golly, Lester," Oscar suddenly exclaimed, "my hat goes off to you. That was a giant step that you took on your own. Harold is right when he calls you 'Smart Ol' Lester.'"

An already hectic trip had suddenly become much more complicated with the heavy responsibility of caring for a little brother added squarely to Oscar's shoulders.

"I guess I should be glad of it all," Oscar said to Arlie, "because Dad and Mom needed a rest from the three of us."

"You are right, Oscar," said Arlie with a smile. "But it would have been nice if Lester could have come along in the first place and not worried everybody so much."

Even Lester agreed with that.

|66|

LONELY WITHOUT LESTER

Now, for the first time in my life, I was without Lester by my side. Weeks went by, and a heavy feeling of loneliness came bearing down on me. Being around Bert helped some, but he couldn't fill Lester's shoes. I wanted to be with my good pal and brother Lester.

I soon found myself wanting to be alone near the river, by the creeks, and in the woods. Every familiar place and thing I looked at reminded me of Lester and of the fun we always had exploring places together.

Then one day a deeply sad thought came into my mind: "Maybe I will never see Lester, or Oscar and Arlie, ever again."

I just couldn't let that dark thought stay in my mind. I had to talk to Mom. I ran home only to find that Mom was preoccupied with a letter, a very long one, that she had just received from Oscar, Arlie, and Lester. It was a fat letter because each of the three had written a lot. Mom was a fast reader, but it took her awhile to finish. I could hardly wait to read it for myself, particularly the part that Lester had written.

Finally it was my turn. I flipped through the pages until I spotted Lester's rough handwriting. Lester wrote first about how big and deep the wild Snake River canyon was. Then he said the Snake River itself was a hundred feet deep in places. From my experience with the Whitewater River, I just couldn't see how any river could be that deep, but here was Lester saying it was true.

Then Lester wrote, "There must be a billion fish in the Snake River. The water is so clear that in the sunlight I can see seventy feet down into it and see some of the billions of fish. Some of the fish in the Snake River are ten to twelve feet long and weigh up to three hundred pounds and are called sturgeons."

Now I *knew* that Idaho must be the greatest place on

earth. I sat back and just thought for awhile about that wild, faraway place with all of those giant fish.

When I got back to reading the letter, Lester told about Oscar's house and neighbors: "We live in a five-room house that sits only a half-mile from the Snake River. Our neighbors here in Idaho are different than those in Indiana. Nobody here ever puts locks on the doors to their house, outbuildings, or their cars. If somebody is riding through or driving through this vast country and is hungry or has to stay for the night, he will be invited in for a meal and a place to stay. If nobody is home, the unlocked door welcomes him in. He can cook his own meal, wash up his dirty dishes, leave a note on the table with his name and address and twenty-five or thirty cents, and stay over the night if necessary, and the next morning be on his way.

"A lot of people here in Idaho are that way. We have already had one man do that very thing when we were all out working on a line fence at the far end of Oscar's farm. His name was Lamar Simmons, a horse trainer and bronco buster. He left thirty cents on the table with a 'Hi Neighbor' note."

I felt better after I read this long letter and didn't need to talk to Mom.

I went outside and watched Dad make a real corncob pipe, using his pocketknife to carve it out and the old grindstone to finish it. When he was ready to try it out, I noticed that Dad carefully checked the tobacco from his pocket to make sure there were no little twenty-two shells mixed in with it.

I watched him load up his new pipe and start puffing away, and heard him say softly, "Now don't you explode." The flowers in the yard were beautiful and we just sat and warmed ourselves in the sun.

After awhile Dad got out his favorite Fisherman's Dream brand fishing pole and reel that George Shebler had lost to him in a bet. Me and Dad went fishing for bass.

"I wish George Shebler was here to fish with me," Dad said to himself as he landed a nice large bass at the mouth of Gates Branch. "Why did he have to fly that darned airplane and try to land it in a thunderstorm and kill himself?"

It was only then that I realized Dad missed George Shebler about as much as I missed Ol' Lester.

Dad caught several more bass that day and taught me a lot about how to catch them. A long time before I had learned how to cast from watching Dad and by practicing on our spacious lawn.

Dad caught eight bass and I caught one. The fish that I caught was so beautiful that I wondered, "Why did I take this beautiful fish's life?"

I had often wondered why me and Lester never caught any bass, only catfish. This time I asked Dad about it, and he solved the mystery for me.

"It is because you and Lester only use dead worms, and only catfish will bite on dead worms. The bass like live food, and they think my little flashing spinner is alive."

The next day was pretty quiet, and Dad and the rest of the family were not home. I could feel some of the same old dark thoughts begin to close in on me, and I knew I had to do something.

I jumped up and risked my life by taking Dad's fancy Fisherman's Dream fishing rod and reel. I went on down to Pipe Creek to fish, imagining that it was the Snake River, and that good Ol' Lester was by my side. I saw that Dad's rod still had a spinner tied to the line and I knew it was ready to catch bass.

On my first try I flipped that darn spinner more than halfway across the Ol' Whirl Hole and slowly reeled it in. I could see the shiny spinner flashing in the clear sunlit waters, and I could also see a huge fish trailing along about four feet behind it. He would suddenly sit still in the water, while eyeballing that spinner, then he would flash up alongside of it, staying about four feet to the side while he eyeballed it again. This went on for about thirty or forty feet.

The spinner was getting very close to me when suddenly the water just in front of me became a boiling mass. The huge fish had struck, and the fight for his life was on. I let him have all the line he wanted as he flashed about in the sunny waters, all over the hundred-foot-wide Whirl Hole.

When I finally landed him, I could see that he had to be at least a seven or eight pounder. But once again I wondered,

"Why should I take this beautiful fish's life?" I just had to set him free.

I couldn't tell anyone of my experience. I had stolen my Dad's best fishing pole that he wouldn't give me permission to use even if I asked him, and besides I didn't have any giant bass to prove my story with.

But I felt really good inside, and those dark, lonesome thoughts had somehow drifted on down Pipe Creek and were now completely gone.

|67|

DAD'S FIRE-TRAP SWEATER

Mom and Uncle Doc and the others had been shopping in Brookville, and when they got home Mom presented Dad with a new blue, very fuzzy light sweater for his birthday.

Uncle Doc gave him a new box of big ten-gauge shotgun shells, saying, "Happy birthday, John, and don't put any of these in your pocket with your pipe tobacco!"

"There would be no room in my pocket for tobacco if I did," Dad said, laughing.

Even though it was August, Dad put on his new sweater, sat in his easy chair, and lit up his new corncob pipe. He puffed away while he read the newspaper funnies to everyone.

One of the jokes was so funny, and he was laughing so hard with us, that he had to take the hot corncob pipe from his mouth to get his breath. Suddenly he let go with a mighty high-powered sneeze, unintentionally aimed straight at his pipe. Most of the burning tobacco flew out of the pipe, with some of it landing on his new fuzzy sweater. The sweater instantly caught fire, and a blue blaze ran quickly all over it. The newspaper in his hand caught fire, too, and Dad headed for the back door. Uncle Doc grabbed a full bucket of dishwater from the big wooden sink and threw it at him. Most of it splattered Dad in the face.

"I'll get you for that!" Dad sputtered at Uncle Doc, without slowing down. Dad saw that the fire was not out and was still smoking a lot, so with a determination born out of fear, he ran out of the house and jumped into the full seven-foot-long by three-foot-deep rain tank, making a tremendous splash. Poor Lummox, sleeping nearby, received a good drenching. He woke up and gave several puzzled barks in his easygoing way.

Dad sat there in the cool water and soothed his minor burns. He still held the Sunday newspaper in his left hand and his empty corncob pipe in the right. A little blue smoke hung in the air around his head.

Mrs. Milbourne heard the commotion and came out of our summer kitchen. She was preparing our supper, including a big cake for Dad's birthday. She saw Mom and Uncle Doc laughing and trying to get Dad out of the rain tank. She thought Uncle Doc had pushed him in for a birthday joke. She joined in by hitting Uncle Doc over his head with a heavy maplewood ladle. Uncle Doc gave up trying to help Dad and ran for his life back into the house.

"This whole family is nuts," he said as he disappeared.

Mom and Mrs. Milbourne finished the job of getting Dad pulled from the rain tank.

Dad was fuming and sputtering. He tried hard but with no luck to get his shrunken, wet sweater off.

"How much did you pay for this fire trap, or did they give it to you to start fires with?" Dad shouted.

Mom knew that the best answer was no answer at all.

By this time Dad was really losing his grip on his temper. He got on the telephone and called the store in Brookville where Mom had bought the flammable garment. He threatened them for having committed "grand arson" on him while supposedly operating a business to serve the public. Mom stood beside him and finally calmed him down enough to take the phone away so she could tell the store owner what had really happened.

"Mrs. Hannebaum," the store owner said, "I'm sorry for what happened. Please come into our store with the sweater on your next trip to town, and we will be glad to replace it with something else of the same value or better." Then as an afterthought the man said, "We will be glad to pay any doctor bills or property damage caused by the fire to the sweater."

"Thank you," said Mom politely. "I will be in with the sweater, and thanks a lot for being a responsible person."

Dad wore the tight-fitting sweater through supper and until bedtime, trying to get it off from time to time, but with no success. He didn't want to damage it or mutilate it to the point where the store owner wouldn't recognize it.

Finally Mom told Dad to lie down on the floor. Uncle Doc held him by his feet so he wouldn't move, and Mom and Uncle Harry got a hold on the bottom of the sweater and pulled it over his head like they were skinning a rabbit.

They had to pull very hard, and when they were finished, Dad said, "I am now probably four inches longer than before, and I want you to look into the sweater to see if my nose is in there. It felt like it got caught on one of the pockets and I can't find it."

Mom had a bad night with Dad. He kept rearing up in bed in his sleep, yelling, "Fire, it's a fire trap! Help! Where is Doc? I'll get you for that, Doc!"

The next day, Mom went back to the same store with the fire-trap sweater in a box and came home with a brand new pair of trousers for Dad.

|68|

SORGHUM MOLASSES TIME

It was getting close to autumn with beautiful cooler weather. Thousands of green trees turned to red and gold, creating a paradise only Mother Nature can accomplish.

Dad, me, and Bert harvested our one acre of sorghum cane. We had nursed it through the summer for the purpose of making a big batch of sorghum molasses. Dad planned to sell most of it in Cincinnati and keep the rest for our own use in making taffy candy and other goodies.

We cleaned and oiled the sorghum cane press and got it ready to go. It was powered by one horse hitched to a long pole that turned a big wheel on top of the press about five feet above the ground. The man who fed the sorghum cane into the press had to duck his head down each time the horse trotted the pole around, or it would knock his head off. The press squeezed the juice from the cane stalks into a big container.

Some of our neighbors heard the news and came with their loads of sorghum cane for us to press. Henry Karns, wanting to be close to Dollie anyway, came hauling in a big load of sorghum cane. He brought it behind his Saxon in something we had never seen before. He called it a two-wheel trailer wagon. He said he had made it at Brookville in a blacksmith shop from the front axle, wheels, and rubber tires of an old worn-out car.

Henry helped press the sorghum cane for us, our neighbors, and himself for about ten days and wouldn't take any pay for his labors, but he did get his sorghum cane juice pressed out free. He said a lot of mushy things to Dollie during that time—they were like two lovesick jelly fish.

Bert, being fourteen, was taught how to operate the twelve-foot-long adjustable cooker and was put in charge of it. Bert kept the fire going under its entire length. The metal cooker was set on a slight angle which made it about one inch lower at its outlet end. A thin layer of juice flowed very slowly through the long cooker, boiling as it went, until it was fully cooked. Then it ran out into a container at the low end, still boiling hot. If a thicker molasses was needed, or a thinner syrup, it could be had by raising or lowering the outlet end of the cooker.

|69|

TAFFY TRAGEDY

When the sorghum molasses making was finished, the six or seven families involved were not satisfied until a taffy-pulling party was organized.

This year my Aunt Annie agreed to hold the party at her house. Aunt Annie, my Dad's sister, and her husband, Sam Lewis, had a large eighteen-room, red brick house with white trim on the doors and windows. They lived about one and a half miles from our place.

On the evening of the taffy-pulling party, eight sets of Moms and Dads, twenty-five kids of all sizes, and three local musicians arrived. The musicians accompanied Aunt Annie while she played on her piano.

After the men passed around the hard cider, the party got underway. Some of the guests started dancing to their favorite tunes until the taffy was cooked and ready to pull in the next room.

In that room there was a large red brick fireplace burning beautifully. It was amazing to me to see how taffy making was done. Two people with their clean hands well buttered picked up a three or four pound mass of warm taffy candy. They would stretch it out into four or five-foot-long ribbons, then double it back and pull it out again to the same length. They twisted it over and over at the same time.

They pulled the taffy many times. The candy picked up more and more microscopic air bubbles, until it became a pale white color. The weight of the candy stayed about the same, but it seemed to increase in volume. Everyone who wanted to pull taffy that night got a chance to take their turn.

Some of the kids were standing close to the fireplace and having a lot of fun, with all of the music that was being played, and with all of the laughter coming from the taffy pullers.

Suddenly we heard someone screaming. A little girl ran

into a long hallway with her beautiful party dress on fire. It looked like her whole body was on fire.

A man who was very fast on his feet caught her, and soon put out the fire with blankets. They submerged her in a tub of cold water as quickly as they could.

Dr. Cupp was called and arrived shortly, but it was too late. The little girl had died. Dr. Cupp said, "You all did the right thing and nothing more could have been done for her."

One of the kids said, "We got to pushing each other to the rhythm of the music, and suddenly she lost her balance and fell into the fire, and that was when her dress caught on fire."

"She jumped up with her clothes on fire, screaming and running," another kid added.

This was the worst tragedy our community could remember. Everybody was saddened, and we grieved this little girl's death with deep sorrow.

When school started up again, a lot of us kids were saddened again, because we missed the little girl who was burned to death while she was in a world of joy and happiness at the taffy-pulling party. This tragedy left everyone with haunting memories for many years.

|70|

ANOTHER INVENTION:
MY FISHING LINE DRYER

In the spring, with school almost out for summer vacation, I began to look forward to getting out and doing lots of important things again.

One Saturday, Dad came in from a few hours of fishing so mad that no one could stand being near him. He carried three small fish and some broken line. I began to piece it together as I listened from a distance. His linen fishing line had snapped and a big-finned wild catfish had got away. He said it was a channel cat, one that sometimes will take a live minnow, like the one he had been using for bass.

Dad noticed that the whole family started laughing, except me. I felt bad for him because I couldn't see anything funny about his story.

After awhile Dad came to me and took my rough and weathered little hand in his, and said, "Let's go where we can be alone and talk it over."

I was glad that he wanted to be with me. We went into hiding behind the tool shop, and Dad stretched out his linen fishing line in the sun to dry.

"The only truth that has any meaning at all," Dad said, "is that linen line, if it is left on the reel wet for several days, will get rotten; that is why I lost that big catfish."

After talking and thinking for awhile, we wandered into the backyard where Mom was using her new labor-saving washing machine. I stood there watching her run clothes through the wringer and saw all of the water squeezed out of them. It occurred to me that the clothes were only damp now and would dry faster, and that caused me to think very hard.

"Gee whiz, that is what Dad needs," I thought to myself. "He should have a tiny wringer mounted on his fishing pole, about six inches ahead of his reel, to wring the water out of the soft linen fishing line before it winds onto the reel!"

The more I thought about it, the more I liked it. A wringer would not only let the line dry faster, but it would cause less drag in the eyelets on his fishing pole. With wrung-out line he could cast the baited hook much farther out into waters where the biggest fish keep a safe distance.

I was very excited now, realizing that I had a new invention that could make my Dad and me rich. I decided to include Dad because he did give me the idea, in a way.

When no one was watching, I looked over Mom's wringer. It seemed kind of simple to me. I thought maybe I could make a tiny wringer with a trigger release on it like the big one.

Now I knew what I needed, and I took off running. I found some one-inch-long pieces of heavy rubber-insulated wire that had been left at our place by the lightning rod salesman. It would be easy to make the two little wringer rollers from this wire.

I ran with the rubber-covered wires to our tool shop, where I locked the door so no one could see what I was doing or bother me. I went to work with a sharp knife and cut off about three-eighths of an inch of the insulation from the ends, leaving a copper shaft sticking out of each end of the two little rollers. These shafts were perfect to fit small bearings on. I did a very neat job on the rollers.

About that time, someone knocked on the tool shop door.

"Who is it?" I hollered, with no intention of letting anyone in.

"This is your Uncle Harry," he answered. My Uncle Harry was a good mechanic, even though I fooled him once by clicking rocks together, so I had to let him in. He really liked my idea, and he started helping me.

In about three days, we had it all done, complete with a spring-loaded trigger release on one of the rollers so it could be popped open for casting.

We used two tiny metal hose clamps to hold the whole mechanism onto Dad's fishing rod. It looked great on the fishing rod, and I was very proud of myself and my new invention. Uncle Harry thought it was great, too.

We demonstrated it on our front lawn for Dad, and we were pleased with the results. Dad was all smiles.

"We have the smartest kid in the world," he said to Mom. "We have a real genius in our family, even if he can't spell worth a darn yet."

Dad put his arm around me and said, "The lawn is not a good substitute for the Ol' Whirl Hole in Pipe Creek. Let's take it down there and try it out on a bass."

We started to walk down toward the creek, and I was very happy. Soon we heard voices behind us and looked back. Trailing after us came Uncle Harry, Bert, Dollie, Mom, Mrs. Milbourne, and our new hired man, Jim MacMullen, an Irishman who had taken the place of Arlie Rust when Arlie went off to Idaho with Oscar. Even ol' Lummox wandered down to see what all the excitement was about.

Everybody around, it seemed, wanted to see for themselves if my new invention was a success or a failure. Not only was my Dad getting awful tired of buying new fishing line, but most of the others were having the same kind of trouble with their fishing lines, too.

Dad was very excited about my new invention. He said he thought it was a great one. But then Dad always said he thought all of my inventions were good, even if they weren't.

After some alterations, the test model of this invention proved to be very satisfactory, and Dad used it for several years.

We never attempted to obtain any patent rights on my fishing line dryer, because of a possible infringement that might have existed against the already patented roller-wringer on Mom's washing machine, where some of my ideas came from.

I made a few fishing line dryers for neighbors, friends, and family, but Dad and I didn't get rich from them. A few years later, new non-absorbent plastic line came out on the market, and my invention became obsolete.

|71|

KILLER WINTER IN IDAHO

I was in the fourth grade now, and felt good about myself for getting that far.

A letter came for me from Lester, and he wrote, "Our school here in Idaho has run out of coal for awhile, and my classroom is so cold that I have to keep my hands in my pockets. You know that I have to use my hands to talk with, and so I haven't said a word to my teacher now for the last three days. I move my head up and down for 'yes'—back and forth for 'no'—and I shrug my shoulders for 'I don't know'—but I will have to give up on that last one because it is wearing out my suspenders!"

I sent a letter to Lester, and before long I got another one back.

"You are talking too much by mail," he complained, "and

I can't read what you are writing because of your bad spelling. Your handwriting is pretty good—I just can't figure out what you are trying to talk about. Why don't you learn how to spell?"

I did work hard on my bad spelling. I really enjoyed receiving letters from Lester, and I wanted him to be able to read mine.

We didn't get a letter from the three frontiersmen in Idaho for many weeks, then we got a fat one from all three of them in mid-winter.

Dad loaded up his corncob pipe, sat down in his easy chair, and began to read this long letter out loud. We all listened with great interest as Lester filled us in on what was happening in Idaho during that winter.

"I have to get up very early and walk one mile to school," he wrote, "and it is awful cold and windy, with snowdrifts up to ten feet high. If we go any place, we have to walk or ride a horse. The roads are kept open to the school at all times up to a distance of three miles in any direction from the schoolhouse, so most of the kids can get there on horseback or walk it. Kids who live over that distance away just can't make it, because even a horse can't get through the snowdrifts. For five or six weeks, no one in our area could get to town, except on snowshoes, for any reason. If there was no food in the house the people would use a jackrabbit or a pheasant or even one of the farm animals for meat.

"The only things that run each day are the trains that supply all the towns with their needs, and sometimes they have trouble getting through the big drifts. One morning, all three of our thermometers read fifty-two below zero. I was two hours late for school that morning. Our three-story brick schoolhouse is called the Russell Lane School, and as I said, it is one mile to the north of us. I always wait to start out until I see smoke coming from our school's chimney. On that extra-cold morning, when the smoke finally appeared from the school's chimney, I started out walking with a west wind blowing and striking the left side of my face. When I was about halfway there, the left side of my face was numb and had no feeling at all. I turned around and walked backwards, putting the cold west wind on the other side of my face. I pulled the big fleece-lined collar on my sheepskin coat up around my head and face, with only the tip of my wool skull cap showing at the top. I started to feel some warmth on my face, and walked on to school backwards.

"When I arrived at school, the big fire in the brick double furnace in the basement had the whole school building warmed up, but less than half of the kids had made it to school. I sat down in my seat, and I didn't feel good. The whole left side of my face was hurting a lot. I put my hand up to see if it was still cold, felt my ear, and it still didn't have any feeling in it. Something came loose in my hand—it was the upper part of my left ear—I didn't know what to do, so I put it in my pocket. I didn't say anything to my teacher—I just put my hat back on.

"Later the teacher asked us kids, 'Where did the blood on the floor come from?' None of them had an answer. A few minutes later the teacher said to me, 'Where are your manners? You cannot wear your skull cap in this building or in this classroom. Take it to the coat room and hang it in its proper place and return to your desk immediately.'

"This scared me, and I ran all the way. My face and my ear, with the frost leaving, were very painful now. Some of the blood was still dripping down from my ear. When I went back to the classroom, my teacher really got scared and said, 'Lester, your ear is bleeding and part of it is gone. What has happened to it?' Before I could answer she said, 'Your face is so red. What is wrong?'

"I answered, 'It hurts something awful and I can hardly stand it. I think my ear got frozen while I walked to school this morning.' Then I pulled part of my ear out of my pocket.

"My teacher turned white. Then she got some first-aid medication from her desk to use on my ear, and bandaged it up. She wrapped her heavy wool scarf around my head and neck. She told me to put on my winter coat and overshoes. She said, 'It looks bad outside, and after you get warmed up and it is warmer outside, you had better go home early this afternoon.'

"When I got home, Oscar and Arlie were soaking the frost from their feet in front of a hot coal fire burning in our little heating stove, and wondering if the wind would ever stop blowing."

We wanted to know more about Lester's ear, but he wrote nothing more about it.

Lester continued: "Our six horses and two cows eat snow for water. We do give them water from the deep cistern, but most of it freezes up in the water trough before they can drink it.

"I think Oscar is getting tired of this long killer winter—everybody says it is very unusual—and of his long walks on snowshoes to the little town of Hansen for groceries. He goes to Hansen instead of Eden because it is only five miles, and Eden is six miles away."

When Dad finished reading this big fat letter, he sat for awhile smoking his pipe and looking out the window. Nobody moved or said anything.

Then Dad made a big speech: "We are fortunate to never have such weather here," he began. "We don't need cisterns for water, and the good Lord waters our crops in Indiana. They can't grow tobacco in Idaho, and that is where the big money comes from for us here in good ol' Indiana. Our livestock would all freeze to death at fifty degrees below zero. Believe me, Harold," he said, ruffling the hair on my head, "this is 'God's country,' and not Idaho, like my brother-in-law Scott calls it."

Loading up his corncob pipe, Dad stood up and said, "Come on, Harold, let's go out to the smokehouse and get Mom one of the big sugar-cured smoked hams for our supper tonight."

We got the ham, and on our way back, Dad spoke in a low voice to me, "I'll be damned. Ten-foot-high snowdrifts in Idaho, and we don't even have any snow yet here. And that poor kid of mine, freezing his ear and losing part of it—I sure wish he would have stayed here in Indiana with us."

We were all pretty disturbed about Lester losing part of his ear. I told Mom at dinner that I believed if Lester had only known what lay ahead, he would not have walked three hundred and fifty miles trying to get out to Idaho.

|72|

A SUDDEN TRIP WEST

Uncle Doc had told Grandpaw and Grandmaw Jones so much about Idaho that they decided to move out there with him. They bought a seven-room house in Eden, Idaho, to live in, and Uncle Doc looked after them. Now that they were there, they didn't really like it, but what could they do? Everyone in the family now seemed bent on going to Idaho, except my Dad.

I was ten years old and the year was 1920. Mom started talking a lot about Idaho again.

"The killer winter," she said, "was one of a kind. It won't be back for years to come or maybe never."

Then one spring day, Mom got a letter from her Mom and Dad in Idaho. They said how homesick they were for Indiana and said that Doc was a good doctor for them, but poor company. They had been living there for a year now. Mom got her bags packed, and then asked Dad if he would go to Idaho with her.

"It's impossible for me to go to Idaho with you," Dad answered. "There would be no one to look after things here."

Dad thought about it for awhile, then talked to Mom again.

"I can't go out there now," he said, "unless I sell off everything and rent our farm to my son, Addie."

Mom was now very jumpy. Her bags and suitcases had been packed for two weeks. She didn't even tell me that one of the suitcases was for me.

One morning at the beginning of my summer vacation, Mom pulled me out of bed very early. She told me to get into a tub of warm water that she had prepared, and she gave me a skin-polishing bath with homemade soap and water, something I wasn't used to.

After that cruel and unusual punishment, I went downstairs where I found breakfast already waiting. Dollie had been up early to fix it. Waiting by the door sat all of the luggage. I wondered what was going on.

The whole family was up, and we ate our breakfast without saying a word.

"What is the matter?" I asked as we ate. "Why are we all up so early?"

"You and I are going to leave for Idaho today," Mom answered.

I almost swallowed my plate.

"How can we do that, Mom? If Dad doesn't go, who is going to drive the Maxwell?"

"Oh, we will go by train," Mom explained, "just you and me."

I sat there for awhile looking out of the window. This wasn't what I had planned for my summer vacation time. I thought to myself, "How am I going to leave all of my animal friends, including ol' Lummox, the Whitewater River and the creeks, the woods with my three grapevine swings, and all of my fish friends that I swim underwater with in the Ol' Whirl Hole, along with the schools of little bass that nibbles me friendly-like when I am swimming there? Most of all, how am I going to leave all of my school friends, including my secret girlfriend, Crystal, and my teacher that I like so well?"

Everyone was still quiet and sitting at the breakfast table. I just couldn't believe that I was going to Idaho without my Dad, Bert, and Dollie.

Then some sunshine broke through my thoughts.

"I guess I will get to see Lester, and he is the one that I really miss the most. And then we will be back home again in a few weeks," I thought to myself.

Dad drove me and Mom to Metamora in our Maxwell, and Bert and Dollie came along. We shook hands with all of them and shed a few tears.

We went inside the depot to wait for the train. Bert wanted to say something to cheer me up, so he took me aside.

"Do you remember the night you upset my bed, and had Dad and Oscar running around outside in their white underwear and shooting?" he asked.

I nodded.

"Don't you ever dare to tell the folks about what happened that night."

"I will never tell," I said, "but it was awful funny, now when I think about it." I started to grin, and that was what Bert wanted.

Dollie handed me a sack of homemade sugar cookies that she had baked for me the day before.

"These are for eating on the train," she said. "I don't want you to get hungry and blame it on me."

Now I felt happier and really began to look forward to this surprise trip.

|73|

I DECIDE TO BECOME A HOBO

The big train soon pulled into Metamora from Cincinnati. Bert, Dollie, and me stood alongside the big engine, dwarfed by the giant drive wheels that looked to be ten feet high to me.

The engineer, seeing us admiring his engine, invited us to have a look at the boiler from up in the train's cab while the engine took on water. Then there were more good-byes and more tears as the train got started.

I hated to leave my Dad and ran to an open train window to wave good-bye to him again, until I saw him disappear in the distance. Since Lester left, Dad and I had become better friends than I had realized.

"There is no need for you to worry," Mom said. "We will be back soon, and then someday we can *all* go to Idaho to live." But I did not see our Indiana home again, until fourteen years later.

As the floor rumbled beneath my feet, it was hard for me to believe that this, my third train ride, was going to take me almost three thousand miles away from Indiana.

The train left Indianapolis and headed north for Chicago.

"Can I go to the toilet?" I asked Mom after awhile.

"Yes, you can. It is at the end of our coach. Look for a sign on the door."

I went there and found the door locked. I decided to walk on to the next coach. I had a frightening lesson in hula dancing when I stepped from one coach to the next, over where the cars were coupled together.

I spotted the conductor and asked him if the train was coming apart.

"No," he answered, "the vibration between cars is caused by rough or wavy tracks." This kind of puzzled me.

"Are you sure you don't have a flat tire?" I asked.

"I bet your Dad owns an automobile," he said, laughing.

"Yes," I said in surprise, thinking that this conductor was a very smart man. "It is a Maxwell, and it has lots of flat tires. By the way, can you help me? I'm looking for a toilet."

He opened the rest room door for me and said, "Don't you have a toilet in your coach?"

"Yes," I said, "but it must be full. The door was locked." He laughed, and several people around us laughed, too. As he walked on into my coach I heard him say, "You always hear the best ones from the innocent minds of kids."

When I finally got back to my Mom, she asked, "Where have you been? Were you lost?"

"No," I answered, "me and the conductor had a very important business talk about train toilets."

"Oh, that poor conductor," was all Mom said.

Soon I decided to jump up and leave again, but Mom grabbed me.

"*Sit down*. We will be getting off and changing trains in Chicago in just a few minutes," she said firmly.

I could tell our train was slowing down from its normal speed of sixty miles an hour. I looked out of the window to a road along the tracks and saw a motorcycle outrunning our train. I told Mom about it.

"That is because we are slowing down and the man on the motorcycle isn't," she said, smiling.

We went a long way into this big city, and then . . .

"*Wow*, what a big house our train just went into," I said, awestruck.

"This is the Chicago station," Mom explained, "and you will have to stay close to me so you don't get lost. There will be a lot of people here. Remember, stay very close to me."

"I will," I promised.

As we got off the train, I looked around. Seeing no luggage, I said, "Mom, where is our suitcases? We have lost them."

Instantly I was lost from Mom. I didn't know which way to go, so I didn't move from that place for fifteen minutes or so. I just couldn't figure out how I got lost.

After awhile, sure enough, there was my Mom talking to a policeman, as they rushed up to me.

"It works most of the time," I heard this policeman say to Mom, "if the kid stays put and doesn't leave the spot where you last saw him."

I don't know how I knew to stay put. Mom explained to me that our luggage was being cared for by the porters, so we didn't have to worry at all about it.

The Chicago station was so big that several trains were standing side-by-side in this one giant room. I could hear trains traveling over us, in the next story up, because they shook the giant building. The ceiling looked to be thirty-five to forty feet high. I asked a trainman why the ceilings were so much higher than the trains.

"The high ceiling," he explained, "was designed to keep the smoke problems down while big exhaust fans suck the coal smoke from the building."

We had to wait in Chicago for a much larger train pulled by two high-speed locomotives. The trainmen called it "The Portland Rose."

We ate our supper in the big depot and boarded the high-speed train that evening. To my surprise, the train coaches were as light as day because they used real electric lights. These were the first electric lights I had ever seen, except for the tiny dim ones on our Maxwell and on the few other cars that I had seen.

Our trip was so exciting that I never even thought of home, unless Mom brought it up.

Occasionally we passed a freight train. I waved real big at the hobos who waved at me first. There were lots of them on the long freight trains. I had never heard of them or ever seen any of them before in my life. I thought they looked so happy and were very lucky to be able to ride the trains so much.

"When I get into college,". I told Mom, "I am going to study to be a hobo and then ride trains for a living." She laughed a lot.

"You will have to learn to spell a lot better before you can go to college."

"I will," I promised, excited to have a new goal in life.

|74|

MR. GOODMAN MEETS HIS MATCH

That night, when I was getting kind of sleepy, Mom told me to lay down in the empty seat just in front of us. The lights were real dim in each coach now.

I went right to sleep, but I was awakened by Mom talking kind of loud. I raised up from the seat a little and could see through the crack between the seat backs. I saw a man sitting with Mom. He was trying to get his arm around her, the same as I had seen Dad do at times, but without trying so hard. I could see that Mom didn't want anything to do with him.

I heard her tell him several times to leave. I didn't realize what this man was trying to do as he kept bothering Mom. She was doing her best to keep from having a "scene" happen and waking up all the people in our coach. I guess she finally lost her temper—she hit the man in the mouth with a good right, and his false teeth flew out along with one that wasn't false.

The man got down on the floor trying to retrieve his teeth and calling Mom names. He touched her leg accidentally, and Mom, thinking he had gone too far, hit him over the head with her heavy purse. Then she called the conductor because the man on the floor was lying very still, knocked out or afraid to move or get up.

The big ruckus woke up all of the people in our coach. Mom had a struggle trying to keep some of the very angry passengers from beating up her would-be suitor. The conductor and two husky uniformed trainmen came and took the man away.

"If it is possible," Mom said to the conductor, "I would like to have a sleeper for the rest of our trip."

The conductor couldn't sign her up for one fast enough. He didn't want another night like this one on his train.

Soon people around us were asking Mom to tell them about the disturbance. She answered the questions that she could.

"He introduced himself to me as Mr. Goodman from Chicago," she told them. "His name bore no resemblance to him whatsoever," she said, and everyone agreed. She added, "I'm so sorry that you had to be awakened in the middle of the night."

Everyone said they understood and didn't blame her.

Mom and I never saw that man again. The only disturbance we had at night after that was the conductor tapping on our bedroom door, telling us who he was, and asking if everything was all right. Mom always assured him that everything was fine and thanked him for his help.

As time went by, I noticed that the men especially liked what Mom had done and treated her with special respect.

|75|

THE "COAL TENDER" MYSTERY

Mom, after being kept awake most of that night, slept most of the next day in a real bed in our sleeper. This gave me a good chance to see the whole train without worrying her. I tiptoed quietly out of our sleeper and went wandering through all of the coaches.

In one coach I could smell food and discovered that the next car was the restaurant. I was hungry, so I asked a man dressed in white if I could have something to eat—like a sausage or a hot dog.

"It isn't dinner time, and you are too late for breakfast," he said, "but if you are hungry, I will make you a sandwich. Sit at this table."

He came back quickly with some kind of a meat sandwich and a soda pop.

"I don't have . . . " I started.

"Yes, I know," he said, breaking in. "You don't have any money. Just sign your name on this piece of paper."

"But I don't . . . " I said, and he broke in again.

"Yes, I know, you don't have a pencil, but that is okay, Sonny, here's one. Now eat your sandwich and get out of here, and come back with your Mother at dinnertime."

"Gee, do you know my Mom?" I asked with my mouth full.

"Are you kidding?" he said. "Sure, everybody knows your Mom on this train—and we all think she is A-O.K. We need more ol' gals just like her."

"Golly, I don't know if I would want that," I said, thinking of a train with a lot of ladies who looked just like my Mom. "Then I wouldn't know which one was my Mom."

He laughed a lot and shook his head. Then he started talking to a guy dressed just like he was, and they both started laughing and looking at me. I got uncomfortable, so I took my pop and sandwich and left.

I couldn't see out very well because I was so young and short among so many older and taller passengers.

"Which way am I going?" I asked one man. He laughed and said, "The same direction that everyone else on this train is going."

He could see that I wasn't too happy with his answer, so he said, "Little fellow, where do you *want* to go?"

"I want to go to the big steam engine that is pulling all of the cars on this train."

He pointed in the direction that I had a feeling was right, and said, "But you can't get to the engine. They won't allow you to go there. And besides, the coal tender is in the way."

Boy oh boy, was I mixed up now. "A coal tender—what is that?" I thought hard on it as I walked through the coaches. "A coal tender—could that be tender coal? That's gotta be soft coal, because one time I heard Dad say soft coal to Oscar when they were shoveling it out of a wagon into a pile. I know that I'll know what it is if I can just see it," I thought to myself.

I walked on pretty fast—I wanted to get to that coal tender and the big steam engine. Suddenly, I fell flat on my face. I had stumbled over a foot attached to a boy of about my size, with a "don't care" look in his eyes.

"*Clumsy*," he said to me as I got up.

I grabbed his fancy-looking cap and ran through the people standing in the aisle. I looked back and did not see him. I quickly sat down in an empty seat and soon I could hear him running toward me. Then out went my foot, and he tumbled to the floor. I stood up and handed him his cap.

"Now we are even, *clumsy*," I said as he picked himself up.

"Where are you going?" he asked, looking at me with more interest.

"Up to the big steam engine," I said. "I want to see what a coal tender is. Do you want to go along?"

"I guess so," he said, glancing back down the aisle. "What did you call it? A coal tender?"

We barely had room enough to walk together in the aisles, but he grabbed my hand and held on. I noticed that he sometimes was lagging behind and acting kind of tired, and sometimes he held on to my rough hand with both of his.

"Why are you holding onto my hand?" I finally asked, stopping.

"I have only one leg," he said, panting. "My other one is artificial and is made of wood."

"Can I see it?" I asked. The coal tender mystery could wait. He nodded.

"Sit down here so I can get a real close look," I said, pointing to an empty seat. I had never seen a young boy with a wooden leg before.

"My foot was hurt real bad a long time ago," he explained as he showed it to me. "I got blood poisoning. To save my life, my leg had to be cut off at the knee."

I felt very sorry for him.

"If you get tired and can't walk very good to see that tender thing," I said, "we can rest here awhile or maybe even go back."

He stood up as tall as possible, and said, "I can walk as far as you can and even run as good for a little ways."

The train had stopped at several small towns, and the conductor said we were approaching Omaha. Mom had talked a lot about this place. My new friend recognized Omaha, too.

"I must go back to my Mom and Dad now," he said, "or they will be after me."

"Okay," I replied. "See ya later." He went back, but I kept going forward. The train went slower and slower, and when it finally stopped I got off and ran back toward my coach to see if Mom was awake yet. When I saw our coach number, I got back on the train and went to our sleeper room. To my great surprise, it was empty—Mom wasn't there. And now what was I going to do?

"Your mother is looking for you." I turned around and saw a trainman coming toward me. I knew that I was in trouble because he took my hand firmly.

"Let's go find her," he said. Soon I saw Mom visiting with a man and a woman. She saw me being led by the hand by the trainman.

"Where have you been, young man?" she asked sternly.

"I was helping a boy with a wooden leg to see the train," I explained. "We went up toward the front end to see what the coal tender was, but he had to turn around and go back when we got close to Omaha."

The man and woman who were standing with my Mom said, "That must be our little boy—he has a wooden leg. Look, here he comes now!" Their little boy was coming toward them by himself.

The boy took a quick look at me standing there with his Mom and Dad and asked, "How did you get here so fast? I never saw you pass me."

"I came back on the outside of the train," I explained. "I ran all the way back to my coach on the wooden boardwalk. And listen, I found out what the coal tender is. It is a little car right behind the great big locomotive that is full of coal. The coal is burned in the firebox to make steam."

Finally we said our good-byes and went back to our coach. Mom seemed to have forgotten all about punishing me for disappearing from her.

|76|

THE MYSTERY OF THE TELEGRAM

"I must get a telegram sent to Oscar from one of the next towns," Mom said. "He doesn't know that we are coming to Idaho. But I don't want Doc and Scott to know, because I love to surprise them. I also don't want your Grandmaw to know because she will work too hard getting things ready for us. Only Oscar must know."

"Do you talk to a telegram the way you talk to a telephone?" I asked Mom.

"Harold, I'm sure your inquisitive mind will soon discover the answer without me explaining it to you," Mom said, smiling.

I have always loved seeking information by asking many questions or by running tests on my ideas to see if they prove out to be right. I had solved the coal tender mystery, and now I was just as determined to solve the mystery of the telegram.

Thinking very hard about how to solve the puzzle, I looked out the windows and thought I could see the whole world. As the train rolled on, the land was flat and smooth and you could see it meet the sky at the horizon in any direction.

Mom and I walked to the rear end of the observation car where doors led outside into the open air. We could see the big rails on the track literally fly out from under the coach and shrink to toy size in seconds as the train flashed over the rails on the flat prairie. The poles and wires strung along the tracks disappeared in the same way. I didn't know that a person could ever see so far in all directions.

Our conductor said, "We are now traveling over one hundred miles per hour at times, on hundreds of miles of track without a turn or a hill."

The tracks were well-maintained and so smooth that we felt as if we were standing still at times. The only sound was the fast clicking of the joints in the steel rails and the roar of the wind.

I never dreamed then that within my lifetime, this wonderful and ingenious way of traveling, that brought East and West so close together, would nearly be gone. Even the poor ol' hobo, who could enjoy travel on the long freight trains and stay ahead of his work, would almost be gone.

Later that evening we learned that a springtime cloudburst had washed part of the railbed away. This forced us to stop and wait for two hours on a siding in a small town while a section crew made repairs to the railroad grade.

When we finally got underway again, the train came to another sudden stop to avoid hitting wild horses that were bedded down on the track and along the right of way.

"The wild horses were very lucky," our conductor told us. "Our train was pulling up a long grade, and that made it much easier for us to stop without hitting them."

I had seen my first untamed horses, running wild and free right outside my window!

There were no fences in most places along the railroad right of way to keep animals off the tracks. Many wild and domesticated animals were killed or injured, but the big locomotives were so strong and heavy that they just kept going.

Most of that night we traveled along the North Platte River, and everyone said we had missed seeing some beautiful scenery. Toward morning, just outside of Cheyenne, Wyoming, we saw a big Indian camp. Some of the Indians were on horseback herding about forty or fifty head of cattle into a corral.

My mind was full of stories I had read, and I asked the conductor if the cattle belonged to the Indians.

"Yes," he replied, "most of the tribes have cattle and goats. They are not thieves like some people think. The Indians in this region are competing in the cattle business on an equal basis with the white man."

We had an hour layover in Cheyenne, so we ate our breakfast and sent our telegram out to Oscar. I learned that the telegrams were sent in code over telegraph wires. When they got where they were going, they were decoded and printed out on little strips of paper that were then pasted on a telegram form and delivered to the receiver. This process was much faster than sending a letter, and it cost less than a telephone call.

I made it back on the train just as it started to move out by running as fast as I could. Mom was not as fast, probably because she had never been chased by the roosters on our place in Indiana.

A trainman grabbed me and pulled me up the steps. Then he signaled for the whole train to stop so my Mom could get on. Our train lost about five minutes, and our conductor said that meant we had lost about five miles.

"If we didn't make it," I asked him, "would the train wait for us?"

"Oh, no, it can't do that," he said. "It would disrupt the whole schedule of trains clear back to Chicago. If your Mom had missed this train, she would simply have been put on the *next* train, and you would be held over at the next stop with all of your baggage. You would be put on *her* train, along with your baggage, and then you and your Mom would be back together again."

The conductor made a special announcement to let us know when we reached the top of the Great Divide of the Rocky Mountains at Wamsutter, Wyoming. The air was crisp and cool there, and I had never seen mountains as big and as high before.

Beside the train track I saw the telegraph wires that had carried our surprise message ahead to Oscar in Idaho, and I wondered if he had received it yet.

|77|

I BITE A RATTLESNAKE

I didn't know why, but I guessed that Mom had a good reason for us getting off the train to stay all night at Cokeville, Wyoming, on the border of Idaho.

She got a hotel room for us, and then we went out to a little restaurant. On the menu was the specialty of the house, "Rattlesnake Meat."

"Do you *really* have rattlesnake meat or is it a mistake or maybe some kind of gag for the tenderfoot?" Mom asked the waitress.

"Oh, no, Ma'am," said the waitress. "It is real rattlesnake meat, and it is a nice break from so much beef and jackrabbits for us natives."

Mom and I ordered "Rattlesnake Meat with All of the Trimmings" for the first time in our lives. When it came, I tasted it and it was pretty good.

"Mom," I said, "I just bit a rattlesnake!"

Mom laughed, and I could tell she was glad that I was with her to share these strange adventures.

She paid for dinner, and then we walked up and down the main street, just to look over the town. It was a typical western town, with cowpokes and Indians and old men who talked out loud about anybody who walked by, including Mom and me.

They mostly sat there on anything that was handy in front of the saloons and told the same stories over and over to each other—and probably never got it right after the first time.

Each one of them seemed to have a quart bottle of whiskey that they called ol' rotgut. They very seldom drank from their own bottle. The tradition was to share with all in the group until there was no whiskey left. By that time they were all so totally confused and drunk that they had no idea who had drunk the most, therefore, no one got mad. However, the last one to get up from the gutter was presumed to have gotten a lion's share of the booze, and the sheriff reckoned that he deserved his terrible hangover and a night in the jail.

Mom and I listened to a couple of their big fibs and then walked on.

"Harold," Mom said, "that sounds just like your Grandpaw Jones."

I just shook my head.

|78|

MOM PULLS A GUN

It was starting to get dark so Mom and I walked back to our upstairs hotel room.

The coal-oil lamp on the rickety old table was turned up too high and it had badly smoked up the glass chimney of the lamp. That made it hard to see around our dingy little room.

"I should have looked for a better place to spend the night," Mom said as she removed the lamp's chimney. She washed it and dried it with an old newspaper. Shiny and clean now, it made a pretty good light, and we felt a little better about the room.

I got down on the floor and tried to catch a little bug that would jump clear across the room when I tried to touch it. Then I noticed a lot of them getting out of my way as I crossed the floor on my knees.

I finally caught one, put it in my closed-up hand, and took it over for Mom to look at.

"Mom, what is this little bug?" I asked.

I opened up my hand. The little bug jumped by snapping its body in the middle and landed on the wall.

"My God!" Mom cried. "We are in a damned fleatrap! Come on! We have got to get out of this hellhole fast."

I had never heard my Mom use such harsh words before. She grabbed our unopened luggage and hurried me out in front of her.

"Harold, you are a little angel for discovering those horrible fleas before we opened our luggage and other things and went to bed. Those fleas are bloodsuckers and are almost impossible to get rid of," she gasped, her voice full of horror.

When we got to the foot of the stairs, Mom hollered for the landlady and shoved me out of the entrance onto the old boardwalk. She left the door open and told me not to come back inside. She started yelling again for the proprietor, who finally came out in a very pretty nightgown.

"I want my money back," Mom said. "The room that you rented to me is full of fleas and we cannot stay in a place like this."

"Honey, you can't have your money back," the woman answered, and she wouldn't listen to my Mom. Mom swung her heavy purse and hit the lady on her head.

Then I saw a rough-looking man come running toward my Mom. He almost scared that rattlesnake dinner out of me. My Mom's right hand went into her purse very quickly, and suddenly she was pointing a gun right at the man's face from a distance of about six feet. The man stopped in his tracks.

"Give me my money back!" Mom ordered them. "Or I will mess up this flea-ridden floor with you."

The man quickly raised his hands into the air and said, "Give this lady her money back!" The woman in the nightgown did it in a snap, and we were quickly out on the street together.

This was the first time that I knew my Mom was carrying our thirty-two-caliber hammerless Bulldog brand pistol in her purse for our protection. I was awful glad she had it out here in this very tough and probably lawless town.

|79|

A NIGHT IN JAIL

We were back on the main street again, and I was proud of my Mom for knowing how to make people get along with her.

We quickly walked two blocks along the dimly lit street, then Mom stopped for a minute.

"Come with me across the street to the sheriff's office,"

she said. "Maybe we can get some help and ask the lawman if there is a good clean hotel in this town."

We found the sheriff, his feet up on his desk, reading a magazine. He stood up and listened politely while my Mom asked him about a good clean hotel.

"Yes, Ma'am, there is," he replied. "Go that-a-way, two blocks on your right."

"I said," Mom said disgustedly, "a good *clean* hotel, not a damn fleatrap. You should give *that* place a visit."

He jumped up from his well-worn chair and protested, "I am a respectable married man, my good woman, and I do not go near such places."

"Suit yourself," Mom said, "but I need a respectable hotel with a good clean bed where my son and I can spend the night, or what is left of it."

The sheriff saw that my Mom was a strong-willed woman who had already had a very bad night, and he also saw that her temper was riding on the edge. He decided that it might be a good time to give her a helping hand.

"Come with me," he said and led us through a back door into his clean, well-kept jail. There were no customers that night, and all three jail cells stood with their steel doors open.

"You look them over," he said kindly. "The beds are medium hard, but are very clean. You have a toilet, a shower, and a wash bowl, and it is all on the house for you and your son. In the morning there is a good wholesome breakfast served at eight, and it is also on the house."

"Thank you, Sheriff," Mom said, smiling for the first time in awhile. "You are so very kind to me and my young son. This will be fine."

"There will be no fleas in your room tonight and no jail-birds either," he said. "I keep a very clean jail, and if any of my prisoners dirty my jail up I give them an extra ten days to think about it while they clean it up better than they found it."

The sheriff left, closing the back door after him.

"Should we close our door so he can't get in?" I asked Mom.

"Oh no, it would lock automatically," Mom said, looking around the room. "And we can't keep him out because he has all the keys to each of the jail cells. Besides, if he finds out what happened in that fleatrap hotel up the street, he might decide not to open it for us in the morning." We both laughed.

We had a good night's sleep in the Cokeville Jail, and in the morning the sheriff knocked on the door and said only, "Come and get it."

When we walked out, the sheriff laughed and said, "You two were very good prisoners last night, even with the doors open. Your escape could have been flawless. Did you have a good night's sleep?"

"Yes, thank you," Mom answered. "I didn't know that your prisoners had it so nice."

The sheriff introduced Mom to his wife, who did all of the cooking for the sheriff and his prisoners. Then he held the chair for Mom and for his wife to be seated at the table for breakfast.

We had put our luggage on the floor by the table, and the sheriff noticed our Union Pacific Railroad tags.

"It is none of my business," he said, "but why did a lady like you choose this Godforsaken town to spend the night in when Pocatello was so close?"

"It may be hard for you to believe," Mom said, "but about three miles out of town, where the train slowed to about thirty miles an hour, I saw a lonesome little red and black sign along the railroad right of way. It was a hand-painted board, nailed to a wooden post in the fence line. The sign read, 'Rattle-snake Restaurant, Two Miles.'

"I had heard about rattlesnake meat being very good to eat, and I thought it might be my only chance to eat some, as well as an experience for my son which he would remember for a long time. I talked to the conductor, and he said, 'We don't often do this, but I will make arrangements for you and your son to get on the morning train.' That is why we got off here.

"First we got our hotel room and left our luggage there. Then we went to the place that was called Rattlesnake Restaurant, and when I looked at their menu my eyeballs nearly hit the table, because there it was, rattlesnake meat with all of the trimmings, the specialty of the house. And it was only thirty cents. And believe me, my son and I have had experiences here that are very dear to us, and we will never forget them."

It was getting close to time to catch the morning train, so the good sheriff strapped on his guns and escorted us to the Union Pacific depot where we waited together.

The morning train came to a stop and we piled in. We found a window where we could wave good-bye to him. As the train pulled out, I heard him holler real loud at us, "Let me know if you make a clean getaway!" Mom and I laughed, but some of the other passengers gave us strange looks.

The train got underway, getting up speed quickly.

"We won't need another sleeper," Mom said to me. "We will get into Eden, Idaho, this afternoon sometime."

Then Mom remembered seeing the sheriff put an envelope in her purse when she had it sitting open on his table.

"I am anxious to see what this is," she said. She opened the envelope and pulled out a picture. It was a photograph of the sheriff standing in front of his jail, his hands held high in the air. A robber held a big six-gun in the sheriff's face, and another robber was removing his wallet and the keys to the jail. On the bottom of the picture it read, "Another sheriff entering retirement without pay." He had signed his name to the back of the picture.

We laughed, and I was glad that we had found this good sheriff when things had looked so dark.

|80|

NEXT STOP, EDEN

We were soon in Idaho, and I was very excited. The train stopped in Pocatello, a prosperous railroad town in a pretty little valley. We had time to walk around the town a bit, and we saw more Indians, cowboys, and railroad men. It didn't seem nearly as rough and tough as some of the towns we had come through.

We made sure we got back to our train with some time to

spare after our experience of nearly missing the train in Cheyenne.

Now as we traveled along, I could see the mighty Snake River from the train windows.

"This river is very deep and very dangerous," Mom said, "and you must be very careful when you are around it."

I couldn't wait to swim in it and was anxious to fish for giant sturgeons. "Just wait," I thought to myself, "until I tell Dad and my friends back in Indiana about catching a super-large sturgeon in Idaho!"

We saw some wild animals on the other side of the river and asked the conductor what they were.

"Those animals are called antelope," he said, "and it is very unusual to see them this time of the year in this area."

After several more miles of sagebrush and desert, we stopped at Minidoka, Idaho, a small railroad town. "The trains can turn around here," I overheard a trainman telling another passenger.

"Mom," I asked, "is this the end of the tracks and does Oscar have to come here to get us?"

The conductor overheard my question and before Mom could answer, he said, "No, young man, this train goes on to Portland, Oregon, but you will have to get on a little short train to go to Eden. And don't forget to get off there," he added, "or you will just keep going back and forth forever, like I do." That scared me a little, so I decided to really pay attention.

He was right—our next train was really tiny. It had only a small engine pulling two passenger cars and a baggage car. We boarded it and went on through more lava rock and desert. We saw lots of jackrabbits, with the longest legs I had ever seen on rabbits.

Suddenly we found ourselves in good-looking farm country. We came to a little town and the train stopped.

"Mom," I said, "let's get off. This must be Eden, where Uncle Doc and Grandpaw and Grandmaw Jones live!"

"No, this can't be Eden, yet," she replied calmly.

Just then the conductor came walking through our coach

saying loudly, "Rupert, Idaho." I sat back in my seat again and let out a big sigh of relief.

This little train didn't go nearly as fast as the Portland Rose did. In a few minutes we stopped at another town. I was so excited that I grabbed one of our bags and started dragging it toward the coach door.

"Let's get off, Mom," I shouted, "this is Eden, Idaho!"

Then the conductor came through again, hollering, "Hazelton, Idaho."

I ran to Mom and cried, "Oh my God, we have missed Eden!" Never in my life had I heard *anyone* talk about Hazelton before.

"We have got to get off this train and go back—we have missed our stop somewhere—and I don't want to go back and forth forever like that conductor man!" I shouted.

I was so loud that the conductor heard me. He smiled, turned around, and came back. He put his arm around me and said, "Don't worry, young man. It appears to me that you want to get off at Eden, Idaho. Well, that is our next stop. The long trip for you and your Mom, all the way from Indiana to the Magic Valley, will be over."

"How did you know that we are from Indiana?" I asked in surprise.

"Well, Mrs. Hannebaum just told me while you were running around so worried about missing your stop," he replied.

"And why did you call it the Magic Valley?" I asked, with my mind now working overtime.

"You'll find out if you stay here long enough," the conductor replied, with a mysterious look in his eye.

"Maybe we will be living in this Magic Valley from now on," I told him, adding, "if my Dad comes out here, too." He nodded and smiled, then walked on through our coach, saying loudly, "Next stop, Eden, Idaho." Before long he came back into our coach.

"Have a good time on your visit to Idaho, ma'am," he said to Mom, touching his hat. "And you enjoy yourself, too, Mr. Indiana Hannebaum!" he said, ruffling my hair. No one had ever called me that before, but I kind of liked the sound of it.

The little train stopped in Eden. I looked through the window at the depot platform and was astonished. Most of our luggage was sitting there waiting for us. I didn't know how it got there ahead of us. It was another mystery to solve.

"By golly!" I shouted. "Mom, look! There is Oscar!" Oscar stood there waiting when we jumped off the train and ran toward him. He had the biggest ear-touching grin I ever saw in my life.

And then I saw Lester running toward us!

POST SCRIPT

To a kid, even the strangest events—like suddenly being up-rooted from your precious home and family—can be accepted if they are full of adventures, mysteries and an exciting view of the future. These true adventures continue on in a second book called *The Magic Valley*.